FABLED ISLES OF THE SOUTH SEAS

AS I.ˢ

ka

AMOTU

oroa

ruka OR

atupe

ki   LOW

ARCHIPELAGO

.Marutea

Anaaiti

.Minerva

Mangareva

Portland R.ᶠ

ista   Oeno⸱

Elizabeth

Ducie

Pitcairn I.

Tropic of Capricorn

⚓ Easter I.

DETAIL FROM A MAP COMPILED FOR *THE ENCYCLOPÆDIA BRITTANICA, NINTH EDITION*, CIRCA 1875, BY REV. S.J. WHITMEE, F.R.G.S. & COR. MEMBER OF THE ANTHROPOLOGICAL SOCIETY OF WASHINGTON, U.S.A. NOT TO BE USED FOR NAVIGATION.

FABLED ISLES of THE SOUTH SEAS

Life imprisons us all in its coil of circumstance, and the dreams of romance that color boyhood are forgotten, but they do not die. They stir at the sight of a white-sailed ship beating out to the wide sea; the smell of tarred rope on a blackened wharf; or the touch of the cool little breeze that rises when the stars come out will waken them again. Somewhere over the rim of the world lies romance, and every heart yearns to go and find it.

~ Frederick O'Brien,
White Shadows in the South Seas

WINSTON STUART CONRAD

FABLED ISLES
of
THE
SOUTH
SEAS

with
insights
by
LITERARY
GREATS

INTRODUCTION *by* JAMES MICHENER

WILD COCONUTS PUBLISHING CO.

That great sea, miscalled the Pacific.
~ CHARLES DARWIN, JOURNAL DURING
THE VOYAGE OF H.M.S. BEAGLE, 1832-36

Strip off your clothes that are a
nuisance in this mellow clime.
Get in and wrestle with the sea;
wing your heels with the skill
and power that reside in you; bit
the sea's breakers, master them,
and ride upon their backs as a
king should.

~ JACK LONDON, *THE CRUISE OF THE SNARK*

Her pursuits were extremely
simple ones: dreaming, bathing
—bathing above all—singing,
and walking in the woods
accompanied by Tiahui, her
inseparable little friend.

~PIERRE LOTI, *THE MARRIAGE OF LOTI*

For my father,
who first brought me to the islands
and encouraged adventure,
art, and literature.

ACKNOWLEDGEMENTS

I would like to thank Mary K. Baumann and Will Hopkins for their creative design; Wylie Nash, Lili Cavalheiro, Angela Esposito, Jennifer Dixon, and Guillermo Nagore for their design assistance; my brother, Barnaby Conrad III, Chuck Robbins, and Paco Taylor for their editing; my wife, Paulette, for typing, research, and computer operations; James Michener for the introduction; Nick and Nancy Rutgers, Paul Kahn, Serge Rota, Daniel Palacz, Teiva Varady, and Julius Rodman for many of the illustrations reproduced in this book from their collections; Stuart Ching and Betty Kam, the Bishop Museum, Honolulu, page 107, lower left; the Bancroft Library, Berkeley, page 28, middle left and center; The Bettman Archives, New York, page 152, lower right; The Metropolitan Museum, New York, page 155; Richard Johnson, page 132, lower; the Musée des Iles, page 113, top; the Musée Gauguin; Michel Boutet for his shells; Mike Bull for the logo; Michael Larsen and Elizabeth Pomada for agenting; Dorothy Levi, The Reasin family, the Daar family, and the Chan family for their hospitality and generosity; David Holden of Colorworks; Pascale Siu of Manuia Travel; Tahiti Tourist Board; Society Expeditions, *Signature* and *Smithsonian* magazines for the trip to Pitcairn Island; Edmundo Edwards for archeological information and expeditions on Easter Island and the Marquesas Islands; "Jungle" Jim McComb for many expeditions throughout the islands; Teihotu Brando for bird watching excursions; Arsene Harehoe for surfing; the late Bobby Holcomb for his artistic inspiration and Rasta music; Bengt Danielsson for information and Marie-Thérèse for her efforts to stop the nuclear bomb tests; vahines of Tahiti for their beauty and posing for my camera, especially, Abanita Tauraa, Corinne Poetai, and Valérie Pambrun; Bishop Morse and brother Kevin Heminway for their inspiration in the belief of Jesus Christ; and my two sons, Anthony and Will James, who were born during the making of this book.

LIBRARY OF CONGRESS CATALOG CARD NUMBER 96-61772.

ISBN: 0-9649701-1-2

PRINTED BY INTERPRINT IN HONG KONG.

BOOK AND COVER DESIGN: MARY K. BAUMANN, HOPKINS/BAUMANN

DESIGN ASSISTANTS: WYLIE NASH, LILI CAVALHEIRO, ANGELA ESPOSITO

PRODUCTION: GLADYS SOTO

DISTRIBUTED BY ACCESS PUBLISHERS NETWORK, GRAWN, MICHIGAN

FIRST EDITION

WILD COCONUTS PUBLISHING COMPANY, 75 WATER STREET, SAN FRANCISCO, CA. 94133

BUTTERFLY FISH IN
THE CORAL GARDENS
OF BORA BORA

INTRODUCTION
by
JAMES MICHENER

THE SOUTH PACIFIC HAS PLAYED A major role in my life, but I left it in 1950 and have been able to return only sporadically. My place has been taken by the photographer-writer Winston Conrad who started living in the islands in 1976 and who now knows far more about the post-war era than I ever could. The son of a gifted writer who had a host of friends in the South Seas, young Conrad acquired from his parents a true artist's eye and pen. Married to an exquisite Tahitian-Chinese girl—one of the most handsome racial mixes in the world—he has made himself a man of the islands, and as such he has reported truthfully on their present condition. Since prose is honest, his camera all-inclusive and his desire to share his vision of the South Seas commendable, he has written a fine book. I welcome him to that splendid coterie of Europeans and Americans who have extolled the islands.

FOREWORD
by
BARNABY
CONRAD

HEN A MAN'S BEEN GIVEN A BAD TIME BY HIS BOSS, when his wife's made him feel inadequate as a husband and father, when his teenager wrecks the car, when the insurance premiums and tax payments smolder unpayable on the desk, to where does a man think of escaping?

Ottawa? Stockholm? Bombay? Tokyo? Pasadena? If he's like most of us, he'll stare out the window and dream a familiar juvenile dream of the South Seas, and in the minds of most men that is Tahiti-nui-marearea, Great Tahiti of the Golden Haze.

Tahiti-ah, Tahiti...just say it out loud....Not "tuh-HEET-ee," the way the *popaa* (foreigners) say it, but "TA-hee-tee," the crisp, clear way the Tahitians themselves say it.

H.M. Tomlinson once observed, "There are place names which when whispered privately, have the unreasonable power of translating the spirit east of the sun and west of the moon. They cannot be seen in print without a thrill."

For over two hundred years, an island no longer than thirty miles and no wider than eighteen has captivated the romantic imagination of men. To describe it, writers have used adjectives and similes they wouldn't dare ascribe to any other place in the universe.

Bougainville declared, "I thought I was walking in the Garden of Eden."

Captain Cook: "Scarcely a spot in the universe affords a more luxurious prospect."

The Son of Gauguin Goes Fishing, painted by B. Conrad in 1960. The church is in Paea. Emile Gauguin holds the bamboo rod. The bearded man is Bengt Danielsson, anthropologist, who arrived in Tahiti on the raft *Kon-Tiki*. He is still there today.

The author quickly adapted to the native life, and that life was wonderful. Others only dream of paradise.

Ancient Tahitian anchor with rope made of coconut fiber.

Captain Bligh described Tahiti as "the finest island in the world ...where the allurements of dissipation are beyond anything that can be conceived."

Darwin: "Far more magnificent than anything I had ever before beheld."

R.L. Stevenson, about the Tahitians: "God's best—at least, God's sweetest."

Rupert Brooke: "There the Eternals are, and there the Good, the Lovely, and the True."

Pretty big words, pretty brave statements.

The great writings in this book by Tahiti-lovers such as R.L. Stevenson, Pierre Loti, Frederick O'Brien, Herman Melville, Somerset Maugham, Paul Gauguin, Charles Nordhoff, and James Norman Hall are more than just the fantasies of press agents. Probably more books have been written about Tahiti than about any other island except England. Though I had read just about every one, I still didn't know what the place was really like, until I went there in 1959 for the first of many visits. Many people go there reluctantly expecting just another Honolulu and are astonished and enchanted from the beginning.

Here's how Herb Caen, a *San Francisco Chronicle* columnist, saw it on his twelve-day visit: "Ever since, Paul Gauguin, the vision of Tahiti has lurked in the back of men's minds like a grain of sand in an oyster, irritating, troubling, always present, always growing, taking shape finally as a symbol of escape, the last place on earth to run away to, a volcanic retreat from reality to real values: love, laughter, peace and plenty. And so it is, even today. As the world grows harder, as the Strontium 90 falls faster, Tahiti remains soft and warm and welcomes you with a kiss on both cheeks."

MORAY EELS AND TROPICAL FISH OF ALL SHAPES AND COLORS ARE PLENTIFUL IN THE LAGOONS OF POLYNESIA. BEWARE OF THE *NOHU*, POISONOUS STONE FISH, AND THE *VANA*, BLACK SPINY SEA URCHIN.

LE TRUCK (OPEN AIR BUS) IS THE BEST MEANS OF TRANSPORTATION IN FRENCH POLYNESIA.

CAPTAIN SAMUEL WALLIS OF THE *DOLPHIN* WAS THE FIRST EUROPEAN TO DISCOVER TAHITI IN 1767. QUEEN PUREA OFFERED HIM A FROND, THE EMBLEM OF FRIENDSHIP. TWO YEARS LATER, SHE OFFERED MORE TO CAPTAIN COOK'S DAPPER BOTANIST, SIR JOSEPH BANKS. UPON HIS RETURN TO ENGLAND, PLAYS AND POEMS WERE WRITTEN ABOUT THEIR AFFAIR.

A TAHITIAN MEAL *FAFA* (SPINACH AND PORK). GRATED COCONUT TO MAKE *MITIHUE* AND *MITIHA'ARI* (COCONUT MILK). *POE* (PAPAYA PUDDING). *I'A OTA* (RAW FISH MARINATED IN LIME JUICE, VEGETABLES AND COCONUT MILK).

Of course, Caen wasn't there long enough to find out that Tahiti is not perfect; for example, I wasn't prepared for the noise of Tahiti. Somehow one doesn't expect Tahiti to be a noisy place. But, there are a *lot* of decibels: the incessant sound of a *toere*—the hollow log used in the Tahitian music; the *swish kerflonk* of falling palm fronds; the plain *clunk* of falling coconuts; the harsh squawk of the omnipresent myna birds; the perpetual boom of the surf on the reef; the shrill beep-beep of *le truck;* the sputterings of myriad motor scooters; the squeal of tires as Renaults dodge squealing pigs; the flopping of giant moths on the window; the rustling of rats in the thatched roofs; the whistling of wind *maramu* when it's blowing; and the barking of yellow dogs. Light sleepers will lament, then curse the crowing of the roosters—nearby roosters, medium-distance roosters, horizon-type roosters—all endowed with the loudest lungs God ever gave poultry.

But you can get away from the noise by heading for the water. Here you forget everything but this new world. The reef and the lagoons are constantly fascinating. Every morning, all morning, I used to explore the endless passes and lagoons, snorkeling the greatest private aquarium imaginable. A school of tiny fish look as though someone threw a handful of dimes in front of you; then one sees long fish, short fish, tubular fish, flat fish, fish as square as boxes, or as round as soccer balls, fish shaped like sabers and others shaped like hatchets, fish striped like zebras or spotted like calico or plaid fish. Some, like the parrot fish, look as though they'd flopped around for a time on Gauguin's wet palette. Some look like a brown stone and others look like Christmas tree ornaments. And then the ultimate, the elegant Moorish Idol:

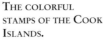

G. BAXTER'S PAINTING OF QUEEN POMARE VAHINE III AND HER HUSBAND, WATCHING HELPLESSLY FROM THE BALCONY OF THE BRITISH CONSULATE AS FRANCE ANNEXES TAHITI. AVOIDING FURTHER BLOODSHED, QUEEN POMARE AGREED TO FRENCH PROTECTORATE IN 1843. NOTICE THAT THE ARTIST DEPICTS THE CHILD IN HER ARMS, NEXT HEIR TO THE THRONE, WITH HIS EYES CLOSED. THIS POMARE CHILD WAS ILL AND DIED A FEW YEARS AFTERWARDS.

iridescent yellow with shiny black stripes, which make it look like a design for a fish submitted to God.

After swimming and fish-watching comes lunch, and what a lunch it can be, especially in a private home: marinated tuna (*i'a ota, or poisson cru,* to the Tahitians), or parrot fish, the freshest lobsters, giant grapefruit and avocados, breadfruit, yams, taro, fried bananas, and best of all, *poe,* the arrowroot dessert (which has nothing whatsoever to do with that mucilaginous Hawaiian paste called *poi).* The food all over the island is generally surprisingly good, I suppose because of the French influence.

And how did the French get there? That's part of Tahiti's fascinating story.

Modern Tahiti's history begins with its discovery in 1767 by the British navigator Samuel Wallis, who named it King George III Island. Eight months later, the French navigator Louis Antoine de Bougainville arrived and named the island "La Nouvelle Cythère."

Captain Cook landed in the ship *Endeavour* in 1769 and called the island Otaheite, because he was told by the natives: "*O Tahiti*—it is Tahiti." He named the windward islands the Georgian Islands, and the leeward he christened the Society Islands ("Because they lie contiguous to each other").

In 1788, Captain Bligh in the H.M.S. *Bounty* sailed into Matavai Bay to collect breadfruit trees, which were intended ultimately to provide inexpensive food for the workers in the West Indies and Jamaica. Then, in 1789, the most famous mutiny of all time occurred, starring Captain Bligh and Fletcher Christian and made famous in the movies and

hundreds of books.

The first London Missionary group arrived in 1797.

The first Catholic mission was established in 1837.

In 1842, Admiral Abel Dupetit-Thouars took possession of the island in the name of France.

In 1880, King Pomare V ceded Tahiti outright to France, which has held the possession ever since.

A string of historical facts do not begin to tell the story of a complex society. Do we need another picture book on Polynesia? Yes, if it avoids cliché. This book does so, contrasting the eternal beauties of the island with the more prosaic, even ugly realities of a paradise losing its innocence.

The photographer and the author is my younger son. He first went to that blessed isle in 1959, when he was three, with his mother and me. We stayed for three blissful months, living in a lovely thatched bungalow on the beach in Paea at the 18.500 kilometer (addresses are whatever kilometer you live on as the road goes counterclockwise around the island). We returned the following year for another three months, arriving by Matson liner. I remember complaining to a bearded, bald man at a cocktail party the first night of our stay: "You know, it took us nine whole days to get here from California without seeing land."

"Well," he answered in a genial Scandinavian accent, "It took me three months without seeing land!"

"How in the world did you come," I asked. "By freighter?"

"No," he said with a twinkle, "By *Kon-Tiki.*"

It was, indeed, Bengt Danielsson, the anthropologist, who had become and still is, one of Tahiti's most prominent citizens and a neighbor of my son.

Raft, liner, freighter, and the flying boat from Fiji via Bora Bora were the only ways to reach Tahiti in those days. But then, in 1961 the lagoon at Faaa was filled in, an airport was created, and Tahiti became easily accessible to the world.

So it changed, but not as radically as we first feared. Certainly, Tahiti lost none of its charm for Winston Conrad who never forgot his early days there. As a young man, he returned again and again to explore its coral lagoons underwater, to surf its waves, and to photograph the many elusive facets of Polynesian life. He took trips to the remote islands on copra boats, crewed on yachts venturing to the Tuamotus, and caught freighters to the Marquesas. He learned to speak Tahitian as well as French and came to know this part of the world as few Americans have. Winston, his island wife, and two children divide their time between Tahiti and the San Francisco Bay area.

One old-timer said recently: "Things aren't as good as they used to be in Tahiti—but then, they never were."

People have always liked to say that Tahiti isn't so good as it used to be; Stevenson stated that he had arrived "just in time." Gauguin was told that the good years of Tahiti had passed, and even Captain Cook complained on his second voyage that things weren't as good as on his first!

But whatever Polynesia has, it is still unique, and colorful. As the following pages so gracefully and so graphically illustrate, it is still one of the most beautiful places left on this travel-scarred earth.

And if for some reason you don't like Tahiti—if the hustle and bustle and traffic of the town of Papeete are too much for you—there are always the outer islands. Recently, my son Winston and I went on a marvelous hegira, visiting some of the least known islands including Pitcairn, probably one of the most difficult famous places in the world

THE FIRST MISSIONARY, MATAVAI IN 1799, SENT BY THE LONDON MISSIONARY SOCIETY. WITH THE REPORTS OF FREE LOVE AND AN IDYLLIC LIFESTYLE WHICH CHALLENGED CUSTOM, EUROPEANS FELT A DUTY TO SAVE THE NATIVES FROM THEMSELVES. THE CONSEQUENCE WAS FATAL TO THE ISLAND CULTURE. THE FRENCH PHILOSOPHER DIDEROT, FRIEND OF ROUSSEAU, HAD SPOKEN TWENTY YEARS EARLIER AGAINST THE INTRUSION AND MEDDLING WITH PAGAN SIMPLICITY AND HAPPINESS; HE WARNED THAT, "ONE DAY THEY (THE CHRISTIANS) WILL COME, WITH CRUCIFIX IN ONE HAND AND THE DAGGER IN THE OTHER, TO CUT YOUR THROAT OR TO FORCE YOU TO ACCEPT THEIR CUSTOMS AND OPINIONS; ONE DAY UNDER THEIR RULE YOU WILL BE ALMOST AS UNHAPPY AS THEY ARE."

BY 1812, POMARE II, A DEBAUCHÉ AND DRUNKARD, WAS BAPTIZED A CHRISTIAN AND CONVERTED AS MANY ISLANDERS AS POSSIBLE WITH HIS NEW RELIGION AND POWER. THE NATIVES, NOT INTERESTED IN HARD WORK IN THE HOT TROPICS, THEN HAD LITTLE TO DO BUT SING HYMNS. THEY GAVE UP THEIR RITUALS AND EMBRACED WESTERN CIVILIZATION; HOWEVER, THEY DID NOT ENTIRELY GIVE UP THEIR NAKED VENUS FOR MARY MAGDELENA BECAUSE MANY HAD A DIFFICULT TIME FEELING GUILTY FOR THEIR SINS.

DINNER, TUAMOTU ISLAND STYLE. TAHITIANS, A VERY HOSPITABLE PEOPLE, FREQUENTLY GREET EACH OTHER "MAI TAMAA" ("COME EAT").

THE FIRST PICTURE TAKEN IN TAHITI BY THE AUTHOR, 1976.

to get to. We also went to such storied islands as Easter Island, Henderson, Ducie, Mangareva, Rapa, and Raivavae.

Yet—once again back at our base in Tahiti—we discovered the truth of that bromide that happiness can be found in one's back yard. As we got off the little ship that had taken us so many hundreds of miles across the vast Pacific in search of the perfect island, we saw it. There it was, right in front of us. Just a few miles across the water was the fairyland of our dreams. There is no one who could fail to respond to the allure of this island. As Michener has written:

...nothing on Tahiti is so majestic as what faces it across the bay, for there lies the island of Moorea. To describe it is impossible. It is a monument to the prodigal beauty of nature. Eons ago a monstrous volcano exploded and the northern half sank into the sea. The southern semicircle remained aloft, its jagged peaks looming thousands of feet into the air. From Tahiti, Moorea seems to have about forty separate summits: fat thumbs of basalt, spires tipped at impossible angles, brooding domes compelling to the eye. But the peaks which can never be forgotten are the jagged saw-edges that look like the spines of some forgotten dinosaur. They stand together, the peaks of Moorea, forever

9468-M

varied, forever new. I once watched them for thirty days, at dawn, at sunset, in the heat of day, and they showed an infinite variety. They were only nine miles across the bay, but in a storm they would seem to be at the very edge of the horizon. At dawn the orange sunlight made them angry ghosts. At dusk lingering shadows made them quiver in the sky. They reached into the air and pulled down clouds; they dressed in gold and purple. If Tahiti boasted of nothing more than these faery silhouettes across the bay, it would still be one of the most fortunate of islands.

POINT VENUS WHERE COOK LANDED AND OBSERVED THE TRANSIT OF VENUS.

There is in the air a strange, pervading peace of mind, an absence of urgency, the removal of the weight of our tomorrows, the lack of striving. We Americans don't realize how we strive; day and night, weekends and vacations, at work or play—socially, sexually, and careerwise we never stop striving. Here the people savor *today*, they relish the moment, they forget the future, they relax and wallow in the infinite delights of nature around them.

EVEN THE MONEY AND STAMPS OF FRENCH POLYNESIA ARE BEAUTIFUL.

So, now you have this handsome, heartfelt, and revealing book. Turn the page! *Haere mai namuri ia'u!* Come with me to the fabled isles of the South Seas!

WOMAN WITH *TIARE TAHITI* (FLOWER INDIGENOUS TO TAHITI) IN HER HAIR, RIDING *LE TRUCK* (OPEN AIR BUS).

TAHITI AND THE SOCIETY ISLANDS

HE WORLD CONTAINS CERTAIN PATTERNS OF BEAUTY that impress the mind forever. They might be termed the sovereign sights and most men will agree as to what they are: the Pyramids at dawn, the Grand Tetons at dusk, a Rembrandt self-portrait, the Arctic wastes. The list need not be long, but to be inclusive it must contain a coral atoll with its placid lagoon, the terrifyingly brilliant sands and the outer reef shooting great spires of spindrift a hundred feet into the air. Such a sight is one of the incomparable visual images of the world.

This is the wonder of an atoll, that you are safe within the lagoon while outside the tempest rages. The atoll becomes a symbol of all men seeking refuge, the security of home, the warmth of love. Lost in a wilderness of ocean, the atoll is a haven that captivates the mind and rests the human spirit.

~ JAMES MICHENER, RETURN TO PARADISE

Tahiti is the largest and most populated island of the Society Archipelago, which includes Moorea, Huahine, Raiatea, Tahaa, Bora Bora, Maupiti, and numerous atolls sprinkled throughout. The people on all these islands consider themselves Tahitian and speak Tahitian, a Polynesian dialect. French is their second language.

ENGRAVING OF AN ANCIENT POLYNESIAN PADDLE FROM COOK'S VOYAGE.

Between 1850 and the mid-1950s, life for the Tahitian people remained largely unchanged; although under pressure from the missionaries, they did abandon their ancient gods for Christianity. Tahitians were their own masters—farming, fishing, and collecting fruit on their ancestral lands—leaving plenty of free time for song, dance, and storytelling. The French government, which claimed Tahiti as a possession, was content to remain in the capital, Papeete, without trying to colonize the districts.

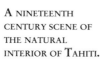

A NINETEENTH CENTURY SCENE OF THE NATURAL INTERIOR OF TAHITI.

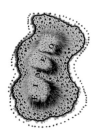

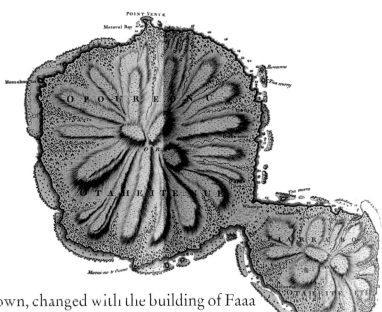

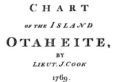

CHART
of the ISLAND
OTAHEITE,
BY
LIEUT. J. COOK
1769.

LEFT: MAP OF TAHITI CHARTED BY JAMES COOK. *BELOW:* A *MOTU* OR "SMALL ISLET" OFF OF TAHITI, OWNED BY CINEMATOGRAPHER CONRAD HALL, SON OF JAMES NORMAN HALL. THIRTY MILES FROM TAHITI IS MARLON BRANDO'S ISLAND TETIAROA.

THE ISLAND OF BORA BORA, 150 MILES FROM TAHITI, PAINTED BY LEJEUNE AND DE CHAZAL ON DUPERREY'S EXPEDITION, 1822–25.

Papeete, a sleepy little port town, changed with the building of Faaa airport in 1960 and expanded into a bustling city. Its growth was largely attributed to the increase of French military personnel to support the C.E.P. (Centre d'Expérimentation du Pacifique), which conducts nuclear tests.

An influx of Europeans and commerce helped modernize Tahiti at an alarmingly rapid rate. With more than 60,000 cars, 30,000 television sets, and a comprehensive welfare system, Tahiti has by far the highest standard of living of any South Pacific nation or territory. The island's budget totals $200 million a year, and to support the civil sector and the C.E.P., France pumps in about $500 million dollars every year.

The average Tahitians no longer farm, fish, or go into the valley to collect fruit, but commute to work and return home to watch television.

Unhappily, Papeete has also acquired the problems of any modern city. It even has its own small ghetto. A writer of a recent article in an American newspaper alleged that Tahiti has no psychiatrists since the islanders do not need them. What the reporter, who was undoubtedly enjoying his vacation, failed to realize is that about four blocks away from the café where he was observing Tahiti is the Vaiami Hospital, the local insane asylum. The people of Tahiti today have more psychiatric problems than any other islanders in the South Pacific. More alcohol is consumed per capita on the island of Tahiti than anywhere in the world. The car accident rate is the second highest in the world, just behind India. The rate of accidents is five times greater than in France and fifteen times greater than in the United States.

Crime has also increased. In 1980, Olivier Breaud, son of one of Tahiti's most influential businessmen, was kidnapped and slaughtered by three French criminals. They had moved to Tahiti on a "get rich quick scheme," captured the young banker, bungled the kidnapping, and resorted to torture and murder—it was definitely Tahiti's most cold-blooded crime, signaling the start of the greed decade.

Certainly with this string of ugly facts, modern day Tahiti cannot be

TAHITIANS PREPARING FOR THE START OF AN OUTRIGGER CANOE RACE. CANOE PADDLING IS POLYNESIA'S BIGGEST SPORT AND IS PRACTICED YEAR-ROUND, WITH JULY BEING THE PEAK OF THE RACE SEASON.

Paradise. But then, perhaps it never was. The ancient culture was not paradise for the *menahune* class, or serfs, who toiled for the king's benefit, and it was by no means pleasant for the unfortunate souls chosen for sacrifices or cannibal cuisine.

Although it is not perfect, Tahiti can still be the best place on earth, where laughter is plentiful and the people enjoy a certain *joie de vivre*.

But above all, Tahiti is Polynesian. Without these remarkable people, the island would be nothing. With them, it is a carnival. They are generous, courageous and comic. They wake each morning to a fresh day that has forgiven the previous day's outrages. In pursuit of money they are irresponsible. In pursuit of happiness, dedicated. They are the perpetual adolescents of the ocean, the playboys of the Pacific.

Yet many visitors despise Papeete. A much-disappointed friend of mine said, "Papeete? What a bust! Tia Juana without tequilla." To those who insist that all picturesque towns look like Siena or Stratford-on-Avon, Papeete will be disappointing, but to others who love the world in all its variety, the town is fascinating.

~ JAMES MICHENER, *RETURN TO PARADISE*

TWO BOYS FROM THE ISLAND OF HUAHINE SEEKING SHADE FROM THE HEAT OF THE TROPICAL SUN. THE TEMPERATURE USUALLY RANGES BETWEEN 78 AND 90 DEGREES FAHRENHEIT

CAPTAIN WALLIS, THE FIRST EUROPEAN TO DISCOVER TAHITI, HAD A VERY ROUGH RECEPTION (BELOW). WHEN HE ATTEMPTED TO ANCHOR IN MATAVAI BAY, 4,000 TAHITIANS WITH 500 CANOES THREW ROCKS AND SPEARS AT HIS SHIPS FOR SEVERAL DAYS. OVERPOWERED BY FIREARMS, THE ISLANDERS ACCEPTED DEFEAT AND THEREAFTER BECAME QUITE FRIENDLY. FOR FIVE WEEKS, WALLIS AND HIS CREW RECOVERED THEIR HEALTH WITH FRESH FOOD BARTERED FROM THE TAHITIANS. WHEN CAPTAIN COOK ARRIVED AND ONE-THIRD OF HIS MEN CAUGHT VENEREAL DISEASE, HE BLAMED BOUGAINVILLE WHO IN TURN PUT THE BLAME ON WALLIS.

AN ENGRAVING OF A TAHITIAN BY LOUIS CHORIS, ARTIST ABOARD KOTZEBUE'S RUSSIAN EXPLORATION.

The first experience can never be repeated. The first love, the first sunrise, the first South Sea Island, are memories apart, and touched a virginity of sense.

~ **R.L. STEVENSON,**
IN THE SOUTH SEAS, **1889**

VIEW OF MOOREA
FROM TAHITI, NEAR
MATAVAI BAY
WHERE COOK,
WALLIS,
BOUGAINVILLE,
AND MOST OF THE
EXPLORERS FIRST
LANDED.

JULIEN VIAUD WAS CALLED "LOTI" BY THE TAHITIANS WHEN HE ARRIVED AS A YOUNG SAILOR. HIS ROMANTIC BOOKS INSPIRED GAUGUIN TO MOVE TO TAHITI.

AFTER SERVING IN WORLD WAR I, CHARLES NORDHOFF AND JAMES NORMAN HALL WENT TO TAHITI IN 1920 IN SEARCH OF TRANQUILITY AND MATERIAL FOR MAGAZINE ARTICLES. BOTH WRITERS MARRIED LOCAL WOMEN, SETTLED DOWN IN TAHITI, AND STARTED THEIR FAMOUS COLLABORATION, CREATING NOVELS SUCH AS *THE HURRICANE* AND *THE BOUNTY* TRILOGY.

HENRI MATISSE VISITED TAHITI BRIEFLY IN 1930. LATER, HE WAS INSPIRED TO DO HIS FAMOUS CUT-OUT COLLAGES AFTER HAVING SEEN THE WOMEN OF TAHITI MAKE THE *TI FAI FAI* (QUILTS) COVERED WITH INTRICATE CUT-OUT DESIGNS. PORTRAIT BY STEIGLITZ.

CHARLES DARWIN ARRIVED IN TAHITI ABOARD THE *BEAGLE* IN 1835. HE DESCRIBED THE WOMEN AS HOMELY AND LATER WROTE, "OTAHEITI, THAT FALLEN PARADISE."

JACK LONDON BUILT HIS SHIP THE *SNARK* AND SAILED OUT OF SAN FRANCISCO IN 1907 FOR THE SOUTH SEAS. *THE CRUISE OF THE SNARK* AND *SOUTH SEA TALES* ARE FASCINATING ACCOUNTS OF THESE ISLANDS.

POPOTI (COCKROACHES) ARE TOO NUMEROUS IN THE ISLANDS.

MOUNTAINS OF
MOOREA IN THE
OPUNOHU VALLEY.

TAHITI, YESTERDAY AND TODAY; FARE TONY CIRCA 1930S. QUARTIER TONY PAPEETE IN THE 1990S.

HORSE RACING IS MOST POPULAR DURING JULY. IN THE *PAREU* RACE, ONE WEARS ONLY THE NATIVE CLOTH WRAPAROUND.

BASTILLE DAY NEAR THE STATUE OF BOUGAINVILLE, WHO NAMED TAHITI "LA NOUVELLE CYTHÈRE" AFTER THE CENTER OF THE CULT OF APHRODITE.

THE MARKET PLACE DISPLAYS EVERY TYPE OF ISLAND PRODUCE. THE MODERN MARKET RETAINS THE PANACHE OF YESTERDAY.

PAPEETE WATERFRONT AT THE TURN OF THE CENTURY. WOMEN CANOEING NEAR THE YACHTS THAT FLY FLAGS FROM AROUND THE WORLD.

THE OLD COLONIAL POST OFFICE. ALTHOUGH MODERNIZED, THE NEW POST OFFICE IS STILL A CENTER FOR SOCIAL LIFE.

PAPEETE AT THE TURN OF THE CENTURY CERTAINLY DID NOT HAVE TRAFFIC PROBLEMS, NOR THE CONVENIENCE OF THE VAIMA SHOPPING CENTER.

LA ROUTE DE CEINTURE, BELT ROAD, WHICH CIRCLES THE ISLAND. IT IS ALSO KNOWN AS *TE PURUMU* (THE BROOM ROAD).

ABOVE: TURN-OF-THE-CENTURY TAHITIAN WOMEN PHOTOGRAPHED AT THE TIME OF GAUGUIN'S ARRIVAL IN TAHITI.
OPPOSITE PAGE: MEN POSING AFTER COCONUT HUSKING CONTEST WHICH IS HELD EVERY YEAR IN JULY.

A few weeks after Gauguin landed in Tahiti, Pomare V, the last monarch died, marking the end of an era. Gauguin spent some time with Princess Vaitua; here is what he wrote:

"*Ia orana (I greet thee), Gauguin,*" *she said.* "*Thou art ill, I have come to look after thee.*"...*Vaitua was a real princess, if such still exist in this country, where the Europeans have reduced everything to their own level. In fact, however, she had come as a simple ordinary mortal in a black dress, with bare feet, and a fragrant flower behind the ear.*

"*It is very kind of you to have come, Vaitua. Shall we drink an absinthe together?*"... *As I am changeable, I now find her very beautiful, and when she said to me with a throbbing voice,* "*You*

IDOLATROUS ORNAMENTS FROM ANCIENT TIMES. AFTER CONTACT WITH WHALERS, TRADERS, AND MISSIONARIES, NATIVES LEARNED TO USE THE PIECE IN THE CENTER AS A FLY SWATTER; THE STICKS WITH *TIKI* ON THE END WERE CREATIVELY USED AS SWIZZLE STICKS TO STIR PUNCH AND ABSINTHE.

are nice," a great trouble fell upon me. Truly the princess was delicious...

Doubtless in order to please me, she began to recite a fable, one of La Fontaine's, The Cricket and the Ants—a memory of her childhood days with the sisters who had taught her.

The cigarette was entirely alight.

"Do you know, Gauguin," said the princess in rising, "I do not like your La Fontaine."

"What? Our good La Fontaine?"

"Perhaps, he is good, but his morals are ugly. The ants..." (and her mouth expressed disgust). "Ah, the crickets, yes. To sing, to sing, always to sing!"

And proudly without looking at me, the shining eyes fixed upon the far distance, she added,

"How beautiful our realm was when nothing was sold there! All the year through the people sang ... To sing always, always to give..."

And she left.

I put my head back on the pillow, and for a long time I was caressed by the memory of the syllables:

"Ia orana, Gauguin."

~ PAUL GAUGUIN, NOA NOA

PINEAPPLES, THE SWEETEST TASTING IN THE WORLD, ARE GROWN COMMERCIALLY ON THE ISLAND OF MOOREA.

TURN-OF-THE-CENTURY HAND-COLORED PHOTO OF MAN CARRYING A LOAD OF COCONUTS.

THE PRICKLY SKIN OF THE FOUL-SMELLING BUT DELICIOUS DURIAN FRUIT.

COCONUT TREES COMMENCE BEARING NUTS AFTER FIVE YEARS AND LIVE TO BE 100 YEARS OLD. THE WOOD CAN BE USED IN MAKING FURNITURE AND HOUSES. THE LEAVES ARE WOVEN INTO BASKETS, MATS, AND ROOFS. THE LIQUID INSIDE THE NUT IS DELICIOUS FOR DRINKING AND CAN BE USED MEDICINALLY BECAUSE IT IS STERILE.

BORA BORA IS KNOWN AS THE MOST BEAUTIFUL ISLAND IN THE WORLD BECAUSE OF ITS DRAMATIC MOUNTAINS AND LAGOON SPRINKLED WITH ISLETS. IN 1942, THE AMERICANS BUILT ROADS AND AN AIRPORT AS A BACK UP POSITION DURING WORLD WAR II. INSTEAD, IT BECAME A PARADISE FOR R & R. MICHENER WROTE *TALES OF THE SOUTH PACIFIC* THERE IN A TENT. THEY LEFT BEHIND 53,000 COCA COLA BOTTLES, WHICH NATIVE DIVERS COLLECTED, AND 157 BABIES. TO THIS DAY, THE BORA BORANS ARE FOND OF AMERICANS.

I saw it first from an airplane. On the horizon there was a speck that became a tall, blunt mountain with cliffs dropping-sheer into the sea. About the base of the mountain, narrow fingers of land shot out, forming magnificent bays, while about the whole was thrown a coral ring of absolute perfection, dotted with small motus on which palms grew. ...

That was Bora Bora from aloft. When you stepped upon it the dream expanded.

~ JAMES MICHENER, *RETURN TO PARADISE*

BOY IN BORA BORA IN A *HEIVA* DANCE DURING THE *TIURAI* (JULY) FESTIVALS. FOR TWO WEEKS COMMENCING ON BASTILLE DAY, JULY 14, THE TAHITIANS CELEBRATE FRANCE'S INDEPENDENCE AND THEIR OWN CULTURAL HERITAGE WITH DANCING, SINGING, FEASTS, CANOE RACES, HORSE RACES, FISHING CONTESTS, AND PARTIES. THE *TIURAI* ENDS WHEN THE PEOPLE ARE *FIU* (FED UP) OR RUN OUT OF MONEY, SOMETIMES IN THE MIDDLE OF AUGUST. *RIGHT:* HELICONIA, CALLED "BIRD OF PARADISE."

Gardenia Tahitensis,
Tiare Tahiti

Nymphaea, Water lilies,
The Greeks compared
them to nymphs.

Calocasia Esculenta,
Taro

Jatropha Integerrima,
Cuban Rose Flower,
Fleur de Rose

Ananas Comosus,
Pineapple, *Ananas*

Nicolaia Magnifica,
Torch Ginger,
Rose de Porcelaine

Allamanda Cathartica,
Allamanda,
Monette Jaune

WATER LILY.
FLOWERS ABOUND
IN POLYNESIA;
MOST WERE
INTRODUCED FROM
ELSEWHERE. *TIARE
TAHITI* (TOP LEFT) IS
ONE OF THE FEW
NATIVE FLOWERS OF
TAHITI.

GERBERA JAMESONII,
DAISY

BOUGAINVILLEA GLABRA,
BOUGAINVILLE, NAMED AFTER
THE FRENCH EXPLORER.

HIBISCUS ROSA SINENSIS,
AUTE. THERE ARE A
HUNDRED VARIETIES OF
HIBISCUS IN TAHITI.

ANTHURIUM ANDREANUM,
FLAMENGO-LILY,
TARO PAA ME'U

NYMPHAEA.
WATER LILIES

PLUMERIA,
FRANGIPANI,
TIPANIE

GENUS FRAGARIA,
WILD BERRIES, COMMON IN
THE VALLEYS OF TAHITI.

LEFT AND OPPOSITE PAGE: TAHITIANS DRESSED IN THEIR TRADITIONAL COSTUMES FOR A RE-ENACTMENT OF A *MARAE* CEREMONY.

The people of the Society Islands were very religious. They invoked their gods in every undertaking, whether war, fishing, house-building, canoe-making or the like. Each occupation had its attendant priests, called *tahu'a* ..., and attendants, who officiated at the many *marae* built for worship of the tutelar gods.... The *marae* were built of stone without cement and were made very high, in parallelogram pyramidal form, or low and square, according to the desire of those who erected them. The stones of these structures were considered very sacred and to them are still attached many superstitions.

~TEUIRA HENRY, *ANCIENT TAHITI*

BASTILLE DAY DANCES IN THE EARLY 1900s.

COMTEMPORARY BASTILLE DAY DANCERS ON THE ISLAND OF BORA BORA.

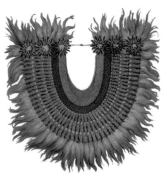

PEARL SHELL NECKLACE.   NECKLACE MADE OF SHELL AND FEATHERS.

THE MISS TAHITI CONTEST IS TAKEN SERIOUSLY BY THE PROUD ISLANDERS BECAUSE THE CONTESTANTS REPRESENT THE BEAUTY OF THEIR *MAOHI* (POLYNESIAN) HERITAGE. THE WOMEN OF TAHITI ARE AS BEAUTIFUL AS EVER, ESPECIALLY WITH THE FRENCH AND ASIAN MIXTURE. BOUGAINVILLE, ONE OF THE EARLIEST EXPLORERS, COMPARED THE WOMEN TO APHRODITE. THEIR BEAUTY WAS SUCH THAT HE HAD DIFFICULTY KEEPING IN ORDER HIS BEWITCHED SAILORS; HOWEVER, LATER, HE COMMENTED, "IT WAS NO LESS DIFFICULT TO KEEP COMMAND OF OURSELVES."

…so interesting; the climate, the scenery, and…the women, so beautiful. The women are handsomest in Tahiti…
~*THE LETTERS OF ROBERT LOUIS STEVENSON,* 1889

Tahitian dancing as seen by Captain Cook's artist William Hodges. The flute was characteristically played through the nostril. One observer remarked, "Must have gotten terribly snotty."

Attracted by the sound of drums and a great quantity of lights, I went on shore one night with two of our mates to one of these exhibitions. We seated ourselves among some of our friends, whom we found there; when one of the gentlemen who accompanied me on shore took it into his head to be very much smitten with a dancing girl, as he thought her; went up to her, made her a present of some beads, and other trifles, and rather interrupted the performance by his attentions; but what was his surprise when the performance was ended, and after he had been endeavouring to persuade her to go with him on board our ship, which she assented to, to find this supposed dancer, when stripped of her theatrical paraphernalia, a smart dapper lad.

~George Mortimer, *Observations and Remarks Made During a Voyage,* London, 1791

Left: Nose flute. *Right:* Tayeto, a Tahitian boy in his native dress, playing the nose flute. Tayeto was the servant of Tupaia, a Tahitian priest and sailor, who helped Captain Cook map the islands of the South Pacific during the remainder of Cook's voyage. Sadly, the two Tahitians accompanying Cook died from fever en route to England.

MAHU (MAN-WOMAN) TRANSVESTITE HANGING OUT IN FRONT OF A PAPEETE NIGHT CLUB. A TRADITION SINCE ANCIENT TIMES, *MAHUS* ARE BOYS RAISED AS GIRLS WHENEVER THERE IS A SHORTAGE OF WOMEN. THE *MAHUS* ARE ACCEPTED IN THE TAHITIAN SOCIETY STILL TODAY.

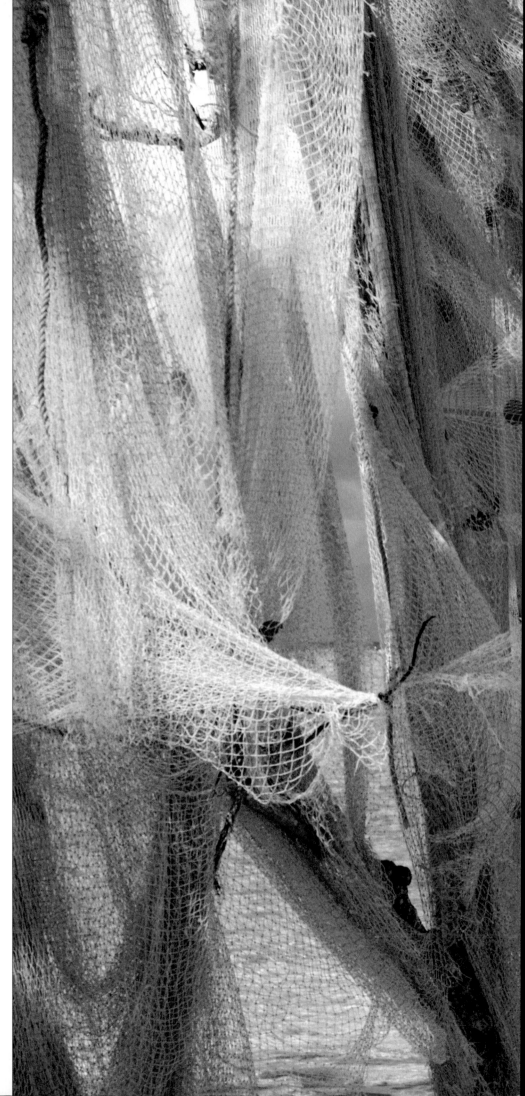

But the Maoris rejoice. The bonitoes and tunny-fish are coming to the surface. The flies proclaim that the season for fishing is at hand, the season of labor. But let us not forget that on Tahiti work itself is pleasure.
~PAUL GAUGUIN, *NOA NOA*

BONITO HANGING
IN THE PAPEETE
MARKET PLACE.

VARIOUS SHELLS OF
FRENCH
POLYNESIA SET UP
ON THE BLACK
VOLCANIC SAND
BEACH OF TAHITI.

POLYNÉSIE "LA FÊTE" R. TATIN

PEINTRES EN POLYNÉSIE
POLYNÉSIE
FRANÇAISE
65F
RF "PAYSAGE D'ANAA" J. MASSON

PEINTRES EN POLYNÉSIE
85F
P. HEYMAN

FRANÇAISE RF

Tahitien jouant de la flûte avec le nez
RF Coll. BESLU 34F
POLYNÉSIE
FRANÇAISE POSTES 1984

Tahitienne et son fils
RF Coll. BESLU 39F
POLYNÉSIE
FRANÇAISE POSTES 1984

Danseuse de Taïti
RF Coll. BESLU 38F
POLYNÉSIE
FRANÇAISE POSTES 1985

52F

POLYNÉSIE FRANÇAISE

POSTES 1985
RF 48F
Marché de Papeete
TAHITI D'AUTREFOIS POLYNÉSIE FRANÇAISE
Doc. C.BESLU

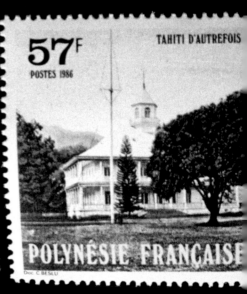

57F TAHITI D'AUTREFOIS
POSTES 1986
POLYNÉSIE FRANÇAISE
Doc. C.BESLU

RF 1F POSTES
FRANÇAISE

RF 6F POSTES
CASE AU TUAMOTU
POLYNÉSIE FRANÇAISE

POLYNÉSIE FRANÇAISE
RF Acanthurus lineatus

POLYNÉSIE
RF
POSTES

POSTES 1984

POLYNÉSIE FRANÇAISE

EDILA

VISAGES POLYNESIENS
"Epoque 1900"

KY PHUNGCHALEUN d'après Doc. BESLU

VISAGES POLYNESIENS
"Epoque 1900"

KY PHUNGCHALEUN d'après Doc. BESLU

POSTES 1985

RF

POSTE AERIENNE

HAURA CLUB TAHITI

27/02 - 5/03 1986

PREMIER CONCOURS
INTERNATIONAL DE MARLIN

LECAM   CARTOR

Roi de Tait

RF   Coll. BESLU

POLYNESIE
FRANÇAISE   POSTES 1985

70F

Homme et Femme d'Otahiti

RF   Coll. BESLU

POLYNESIE
FRANÇAISE   POSTES 1985

55F

Polynésie Française

22F

VISAGES POLYNESIENS
"Epoque 1900"

KY PHUNGCHALEUN d'après Doc. BESLU

POSTES 1985

RF

POLYNÉSIE FRANÇAISE
RF

POSTES 1985

TAHITI D'AUTREFOIS: Tahitiennes de Papeete

Doc. C BESLU   45

du Roi à Papeete

RF

EDILA

42F
POSTES 1985

TAHITI D'AUTREFOIS: Entrée de la Ville de Papeete

POLYNÉSIE FRANÇAISE   RF

Doc. C BESLU

56F
POSTES 1986

TAHITI D'AUTREFOIS:
Pêche au Harpon

POLYNÉSIE FRANÇAISE   RF

Doc. C BESLU   EDILA

FRANÇAISE   12F

POSTES 1985

POLYNESIE FRANÇAISE
400F   RF

AERIENNE 1986

POLYNESIE FRANÇAISE

150F

Point Venus
Matavai Bay

OPOUREONU
OR
OTAHEITE-NUE

TIARRABOU OR
OTAHEITE-ETE

D. KARL SOLANDER

RF

"I tell you, the only leper I ever
knew that made me cry was a
kid. I used to see on the porch of
a house on the road to Papara
from Papeete a big doll. A little
leper girl owned it, and she was
ashamed to be seen outside her
home, so she put on the veranda
the doll she loved best to greet
her friends. She made out that
the doll was really herself, and
she loved to listen when those
who might have been playmates
talked to the doll and fondled it.
She lived for and in the doll, and
those who cherished the little
girl saw that each Christmas the
doll was exchanged secretly for a
bigger one, keeping pace with
the growth of the child. I have
caressed it and sung to it, and
guessed that the child was
peeping and listening inside. She
herself never touched it, for it
would be like picking up one's
own self. Each Christmas she
saw herself born again, for the
old dolls were burned without
her knowledge. And all the time
her own little body was falling
to pieces. Last Christmas she
was carried to the door to see
the new doll. I bought it for her,
and I had in it a speaking-box,
to say *'Bonjour!'* I sent to Paris
for it. She's dead now, poor little
devil, or they'd have shut her up
in the lazaretto."

~ FREDERICK O'BRIEN,
MYSTIC ISLES OF THE SOUTH SEAS

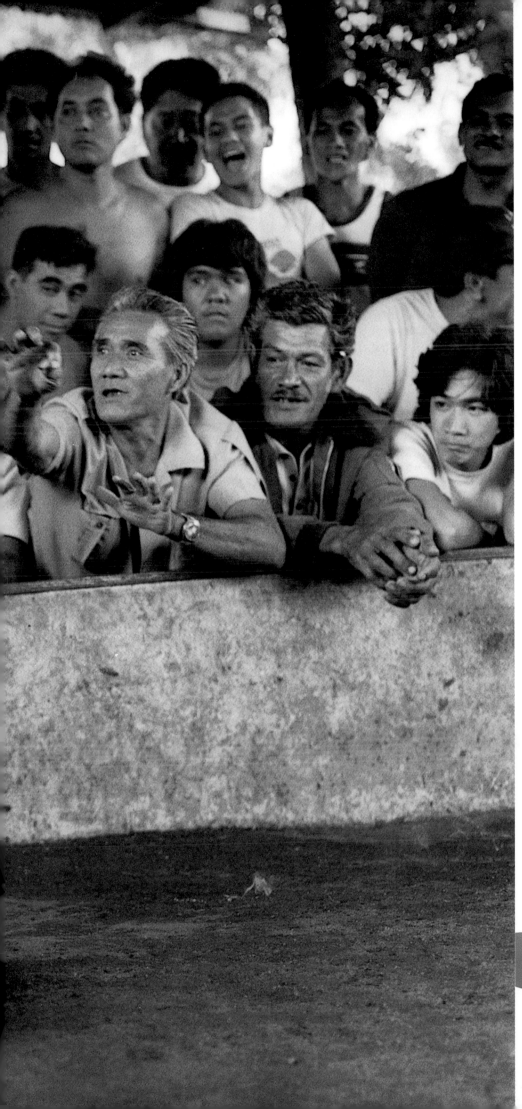

Fitted for battle by generations of skilled selective breeding, the two cocks eyed each other warily, crouching beak to beak with hackles raised. The Taio bird attacked. They buckled in mid-air. They crouched, bloody and panting, only to leap together once more, to contend with a skill and pertinacity that brought low-voiced exclamations from the crowd.... *"Aué tatou é!"*

CHARLES NORDHOFF, *NO MORE GAS*

Those young women were well called *les belles Tahitiennes.* Their skins were like pale-brown satin, but exceeding all their other charms were their lustrous eyes…. They were the eyes of children of the sun, eyes that had stirred disciplined seamen to desertion, eyes that had burned ships, and created the mystery of the *Bounty,* eyes of enchantresses of the days of Helen.

~ FREDERICK O'BRIEN,
MYSTIC ISLES OF THE SOUTH SEAS

Cotton candy being sold at *les barraques* along the Papeete waterfront during *La Fête du Tiurai*. Concession stands are set up as in any small town carnival, but they have a Polynesian flair.

Nuclear bomb test on Fangataufa atoll, near Moruroa, 750 miles from Tahiti. Starting in 1966, forty atmospheric atomic bomb tests, including five hydrogen bombs, were conducted there. In 1973, the military switched to underground testing. The coral reefs now resemble large pieces of swiss cheese. Lucrative jobs with the C.E.P. brought many changes to life in Tahiti. Many Polynesians gave up their quiet islands to move to the bright lights of the city. Paris introduced a moratorium in 1992; however, President Chirac approved more nuclear tests in 1995. People worldwide protested and violence broke out on the streets of Tahiti. Unfortunately, the nuclear waste remains.

Then his body erect, his eyes toward the stars, augustly, and without hesitation or choice of footprints, the *tahua* walked upon the *umu.* His body was naked except for the *tapa,* which extended from his shoulders to his knees....

...A thermometer held over the *umu* of Papa Ita at a height of six feet registered 282 degrees Fahrenheit.... No precaution was taken by the walkers. I knew most of them intimately. There was no fraud, no ointment or oil or other application to the feet, and all had not the same thickness of sole.

~ Frederick O'Brien,
Mystic Isles of the South Seas

Opposite page: The mysterious, ancient art of fire-walking is still practiced by *tahua* (shaman).

Tahiti is very far away, and I knew
that I should never see it again.
A chapter of my life was closed, and I felt
a little nearer to inevitable death.
~ W. SOMERSET MAUGHAM, *The Moon and Sixpence*

AUSTRAL ISLANDS
ISLANDS OF PASSION

HE AUSTRAL ISLANDS CONSIST OF TUBUAI, RURUTU, Rapa, Rimatara, and Raivavae. Raivavae, sometimes called the Island of Passion, was once the most fascinating and mysterious island in Polynesia. The island's society was based primarily on war and sex.

Today, life in Raivavae hardly resembles the ancient culture. A high island 400 miles from Tahiti, Raivavae is inhabited by 1,300 church-going Christians who keep their village clean, are industrious, and are teetotalers except during the July festivals and Christmas holidays. During the vacations, they party for days, eating lavishly and drinking alcohol and home-made orange beer, until not a drop of liquor is left on the island. The rest of the year, they go to church *every* day, even twice a day.

In 1819, King Pomare came to the Australs and converted the people to Christianity, but not before Pomare's group had participated in one of the last lustful feasts. Pomare and his missionaries could not resist the allurement of such a strong Polynesian culture, much to the chagrin of the other missionaries. Under Pomare's direction, the people of Raivavae soon embraced Christianity with as much enthusiasm as they had their pagan religion. King Pomare died a few years later of drink. Today, the churches dominate the people's lives as thoroughly as the stone temples of their ancient religion once had. The Christianity they practice today is almost identical to that first taught to King Pomare by the London Missionary Society.

By 1830, because of diseases that reached them from nearby Tubuai, only 120 people were left, compared to the 3,000 who had greeted Pomare's arrival. Because Polynesian history is an oral tradition, much

TOP: THE AUSTRAL WOMEN EXCEL AT SEWING *TI FAI FAI* (QUILTS OF INTRICATE CUT-OUT DESIGNS). THESE INSPIRED HENRI MATISSE TO DO HIS FAMOUS CUT-OUT COLLAGES. *BOTTOM:* POLYNESIAN GIRLS PHOTOGRAPHED AT THE TURN OF THE CENTURY.

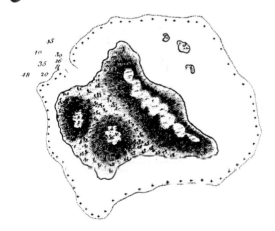

knowledge of their ancient customs disappeared with the deaths of so many people.

Fortunately, research in the 1930s by J. Frank Stimson, and in 1957 by Dr. Donald Marshall, tells us about the customs of ancient Raivavae. By interviewing various old natives and comparing stories along with archeological finds, Stimson and Marshall have pieced together the story of the exotic rituals of Raivavae. Their *marae*, more lavishly built than most Polynesian islands, were surrounded by stone phalluses and some had statues of women in various stages of pregnancy.

In ancient Raivavae society, the male children were brought up as warriors. Their genitals were massaged with special unguents to give the boys virility and to make them brave in battle. The women were raised for procreation and pleasures in sex. One of the unusual customs of Raivavae required the mothers or grandmothers to massage girls' clitorises and tie them with fibers so that the clitoris would become enlarged. With the girls' coming of age, a priest would inspect and measure their clitoris with an instrument made of rosewood, to see if the clitoris had reached an ideal size, suitable for the young warriors.

Archeologists found a special bench for the girls known as a "stone inspection seat." There were even *marae* complete with disrobing rooms.

The *marae* of Raivavae, once the hotbed of orgies where sex was performed publicly, are now toppled and covered by the thick jungle. Some of the stones were used as the foundations for Christian churches. The people of Raivavae and Tahiti still fear their ancient gods and the *mana* or power of the old statues.

There are many stories of bad luck occasioned by tampering with the *tiki* or stone images of the gods. In the mid-1950s, an engineer named Steve Higgins moved two large statues, a female eight feet high and five feet thick, and a male statue six feet by three feet, to Papeete. Not long afterwards, he died. The superstitious locals blame his death on the voodoo-like curse of the *tiki*.

Today, one of these *tiki* can be seen in the garden of the Gauguin Museum on Tahiti. However, the people of Raivavae are now demanding that the *tiki* be returned to their island to restore their *mana*.

It is necessary for the European to rid his mind of associations of nastiness in dealing with these matters, and to remember that the Polynesian receives the facts connected with the handing on of human life with the same simple candour as the phenomena observed in his garden or anywhere else'.

To the Polynesians the sexual act is just as simple and natural as eating and drinking, and therefore they can talk of it in the same unembarrassed and direct manner. 'It is necessary for the European to rid his mind of associations of nastiness in dealing with these matters, and to remember that the Polynesian receives the facts connected with the handing on of human life with the same simple candour as the phenomena observed in his garden or anywhere else'.

~ E.E.V. Collocott, *Marriage in Tonga*,
Journal of the Polynesian Society, No. 4, 1923.

Above: The Austral islanders excel at carving miniature wooden canoes. *Left:* Spear fishermen on the reef.

It is not surprising in the circumstances that most of the well-known complexes and maladjustments from which our children suffer are still unknown in Polynesia; I have not yet been able to discover any serious cases of thumb-sucking, contrariness, bed-wetting, day-dreaming, nervousness, nail-biting or stuttering on the islands, where I have lived long enough to know the conditions well. Not even of the well-known Oedipus complex is there a trace. According to Freud, as is known, this complex (or at least conflict situation) is a universal phenomenon, but the validity of this theory, as with so many other theories of Freud's, is in fact restricted to communities where the conditions are identical with those of the Austrian middle class at the turn of the century.

If it sometimes happens in Western countries that a boy takes a sexual interest in his mother and is hostile to his father, this is of course due to our special conditions. With us (1) all sex relations between youths are forbidden; this creates an unhealthy interest which expresses itself in peculiar ways, (2) parental discipline is severe, and (3) is exercised primarily by the father, towards whom, therefore, a spirit of opposition easily arises in the son. With the unlimited sexual liberty which the children enjoy in Polynesia, and the scanty parental discipline, the main preliminary conditions for a complex of this kind are removed altogether. Moreover, a Polynesian child has always more than one mother and father, which makes the staging of a classical triangle drama absolutely impossible.

~ Bengt Danielsson, *Love in the South Seas*, 1956

FISHING FROM
OUTRIGGER CANOES IS
COMMON
THROUGHOUT THE
MANY LAGOONS OF
POLYNESIA.

...not only do their feet dance, but their arms, hands, fingers, ay, their very eyes seem to dance in their heads.
~ HERMAN MELVILLE, *Typee*, 1842

DANCERS ON THE ISLAND OF RAPA, THE SOUTHERNMOST ISLAND OF THE AUSTRAL ARCHIPELAGO.

A BURIAL *MARAE* AS SEEN IN THE EIGHTEENTH CENTURY BY CAPTAIN COOK'S ARTIST WILLIAM HODGES.
OPPOSITE PAGE: A REENACTMENT OF ANCIENT CUSTOMS AT MARAE ARAHURAHU, IN TAHITI, GIVES A GOOD IMPRESSION OF WHAT A TYPICAL *MARAE* SCENE IN ANCIENT RAIVAVAE WOULD HAVE LOOKED LIKE.

As this terribly earnest procession arrived, the canoes were quietly drawn up along the shore, and the guests were met at the receiving *marae* by an imposing procession of the dignitaries and warriors of the land grandly attired, and also unarmed, headed by the king, the two primates, Paoa-uri and Paoa-tea, and the priests of the realm, who greeted them in low, solemn

TIKI ARE STONE OR WOOD-CARVED IDOLATROUS STATUES, FASHIONED IN THE IMAGES OF ANCIENT POLYNESIAN GODS.

tones. Then everybody alike set to work silently disposing of the sacrifices just arrived, combined with others of the same mixed kind prepared by the inhabitants of the land. They strung them through the heads with sennit, an act called *tu'i-aha*, and then suspended them upon the boughs of the trees of the seaside and inwards, the fish diversifying the ghastly spectacle of the human bodies, a decoration called *ra'a nu'u a 'Oromata-'oa* (sacredness of the host of Warrior-of-long-face).... Upon the road that led up to the inner *marae* were then laid as rollers, called *ra'o*, the bodies of slain men, and over them were drawn the canoes still containing idols and precious things,... Then the high priest concluded the inauguration ceremony by plucking out the eye of one more human victim and proffering it to the sovereign, who made a semblance to receive and swallow it, but in reality did not touch it. This was intended to give keen perception and farsightedness to the recipient and was called *pivai-ari'i* (apart-with sovereign).

~ Teuira Henry, *Ancient Tahiti*, 1848

The image of a face is carved on this porous volcanic rock.

LEFT: THERE ARE DOZENS OF TYPES OF BANANAS IN POLYNESIA. SOME, SUCH AS THE *FEI* (MOUNTAIN BANANAS), MUST BE COOKED BEFORE EATING. *HA MOA* BANANAS, SUCH AS THE ONES THE MAN IS CARRYING ON THE LEFT, ARE THE SWEETEST.

TOP RIGHT: A YOUNG GIRL ON A DOORSTEP IN RAPA. *CENTER:* A STRING OF SWEET TASTING *I'IHI* OR *ROUGET* FISH. *RIGHT:* AN ABUNDANCE OF GREEN GRASS MAKES A PARADISE FOR CATTLE.

In these genial regions, one's wants are naturally diminished; and those which remain are easily gratified: fuel, house-shelter, and, if you please, clothing, may be entirely dispensed with.

~ HERMAN MELVILLE, *OMOO,* 1843

AMO OFA'I (ROCK LIFTING) IS A FAVORITE SPORT AMONG AUSTRAL ISLANDERS. SOME OF THE PARTICIPANTS RESEMBLE SUMO WRESTLERS AND LIFT ROCKS WEIGHING UP TO 130 KILOS. KEEPING A FIRM GRIP ON THE ROCK AND THEN LIFTING IT ONTO ONE'S SHOULDER MAKES IT HARDER AND MORE INTERESTING THAN REGULAR WEIGHT LIFTING. THE CONTESTANTS ARE ALLOWED TO CHOOSE ANY OF THE ROCKS PROVIDED AND MAY MAKE NUMEROUS ATTEMPTS TO LIFT THEM. IT IS A SIMPLE SPORT: THE PERSON WHO LIFTS THE HEAVIEST ROCK ONTO HIS SHOULDER IS THE WINNER.

BELOW: GIRL ON THE ISLAND OF RAPA, HOLDING STRINGS WHICH RESEMBLE THE CAT'S CRADDLE. THIS GAME WAS OBSERVED BY THE EARLY EXPLORERS IN THE BEGINNING OF THE NINETEENTH CENTURY. AS THE ISLANDERS PLAY THE GAME, THEY RECITE OLD STORIES AND DISCUSS THEIR LINEAGE.

PITCAIRN ISLANDS HOME OF THE BOUNTY MUTINEERS

APTAIN BLIGH, NAKED EXCEPT FOR HIS SHIRT, AND *with his hands tied behind his back, was standing by the mizzenmast. Christian stood before him, holding in one hand the end of the line by which Bligh was bound and in the other a bayonet, and around them were several of the able seamen, fully armed,.... In the confusion we made our way aft a little way, and as we approached the spot where Bligh was standing, I heard Christian say, "Will you hold your tongue, sir, or shall I force you to hold it? I'm master of this ship now, and, by God, I'll stand no more of your abuse!" Sweat was pouring down Bligh's face. He had been making a great outcry, shouting, "Murder! Treason!" at the top of his voice.*

"Master of my ship, you mutinous dog!" he yelled. "I'll see you hung! I'll have you flogged to ribbons! I'll . . ."

"Mamu, sir! Hold your tongue or you are dead this instant!"

Christian placed the point of his bayonet at Bligh's throat with a look in his eye there was no mistaking. "Slit the dog's gullet!" someone shouted; and there were cries of "Let him have it, Mr. Christian!" "Throw him overboard!" "Feed the bastard to the sharks!" and the like. It was only then, I think, that Captain Bligh realized his true situation.

~ CHARLES NORDHOFF AND JAMES NORMAN HALL, MUTINY ON THE BOUNTY

BELOW: A MAP OF PITCAIRN ISLAND DRAWN AT ITS DISCOVERY DURING CAPTAIN CARTERET'S VOYAGE IN 1767. PITCAIRN WAS THE SAILOR WHO FIRST SPOTTED THE ISLAND, WHICH IS ABOUT 4,000 MILES WEST OF CHILE AND ABOUT 2,500 MILES SOUTHEAST OF TAHITI.

RIGHT: WILLIAM BLIGH'S LOG BOOK AND HALF A COCONUT SHELL, WHICH ACCOMPANIED HIM ON THE LONG OPEN BOAT VOYAGE TO TIMOR.

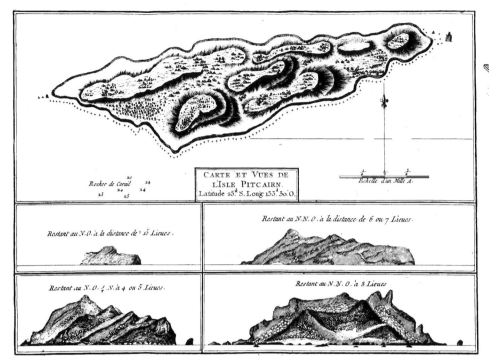

On April 28, 1789, when H.M.S. *Bounty* was near the Tonga group on her way home from Tahiti with a cargo of breadfruit trees for planting in the West Indies, the master's mate Fletcher Christian and others of the crew mutinied. They cast adrift Lieutenant William Bligh and eighteen loyal sailors in a twenty-three-foot launch and sailed for Tahiti where they dropped off fourteen sailors. Some were loyalists who could not fit into the launch with Bligh and others were mutineers who decided to stay on Tahiti. After an unsuccessful attempt at settling on Tubuai in the Austral Island group, Christian, along with nine of the mutineers, six Tahitian men, and twelve Tahitian women, eventually found the little known island of Pitcairn in 1790. Pitcairn was remote and inaccessible, but the ancient Polynesians who had once lived there left the island planted with many coconuts and breadfruit; in sum, it was a paradisiacal hideaway.

But paradise did not last for long. A few years after their settlement, the Tahitians revolted against the English and killed all the men except Young, Adams, Quintal, and McCoy. Eventually, McCoy learned to make a potent liquor from *ti* plants and became so demented that he drowned himself. Quintal also went insane and had to be killed by Young and Adams in self-defense. Captain Edward Edwards, sent from England to Tahiti, found fourteen *Bounty* sailors who had remained there. He wrecked the *Pandora* on a reef and let four *Bounty* seamen drown in a prison on deck known as "Pandora's Box"; they were still in manacles. Finally in 1792, ten mutineers were brought to

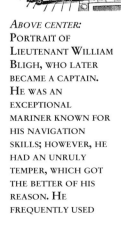

ABOVE CENTER: PORTRAIT OF LIEUTENANT WILLIAM BLIGH, WHO LATER BECAME A CAPTAIN. HE WAS AN EXCEPTIONAL MARINER KNOWN FOR HIS NAVIGATION SKILLS; HOWEVER, HE HAD AN UNRULY TEMPER, WHICH GOT THE BETTER OF HIS REASON. HE FREQUENTLY USED PROFANITY WHILE REPRIMANDING HIS SAILORS AND OFFICERS.

ABOVE BOTTOM: FLETCHER CHRISTIAN HOLDING A PISTOL TO BLIGH ON THE MORNING OF THE FAMOUS MUTINY. THE PREVIOUS DAY, BLIGH HAD RUDELY ACCUSED CHRISTIAN OF STEALING HIS COCONUTS.

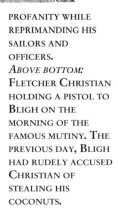

trial in Newgate; three were hanged. In 1800, Young died of asthma, leaving John Adams the only man among nine women and twenty-five children. Known to all the islanders as "Father," John Adams was the head of the community, guided by the virtues of the Church of England's Book of Common Prayer.

In 1808 when Captain Folger of the American sealing ship *Topaz* discovered the thirty-five people on Pitcairn, he could hardly believe that this idyllic community had been started by the *Bounty* mutineers.

In 1814, ignorant of the American discovery of Pitcairn, the British ships *Briton* and *Tagus* rediscovered the island. Twenty-five years had passed since the mutiny of the *Bounty*, but John Adams still feared he might be tried by court in England. Upon finding Adams such a kind, determined leader, the British commander assured him it would be "an act of great cruelty and inhumanity to arrest him."

Because of fear of overcrowding, the Pitcairners unsuccessfully tried to settle on Tahiti in 1831. Lacking immunities, ten Pitcairners died within a few months, including Thursday October Christian, who was Fletcher Christian's son, the first child born on Pitcairn and the oldest member of the community. Incidentally, Christian named his son Thursday October because he was born on a Thursday in October. Thursday changed his name to Friday when he discovered twenty-four years later that the mutineers had made a mistake in the calendar. The people missed their island and quickly returned to it, and by 1856, the islanders numbered 194. With British aid, they settled on the uninhabited island of Norfolk; however, some of the islanders were homesick and in 1859 returned to their island just in time to stop the French from annexing it.

In 1887, the Pitcairners became Seventh Day Adventists, although they did not have to change their lifestyle since most were abstainers and non-smokers. However, they killed all the pigs on the island to remove the temptation to eat pork.

Since all the children in the first generation were descended from six of the mutineers, relationships are, as Mark Twain phrased it, "wonderfully, even astoundingly, mixed up and complicated." He couldn't resist writing this in the story *The Great Revolution in Pitcairn*—and it is not all that exaggerated:

A stranger, for instance, says to an islander,

"You speak of that young woman as your cousin; a while ago you called her your aunt."

TOP: BOUNTY BAY SKETCHED IN 1825 BY F.W. BEECHEY, CAPTAIN OF THE *BLOSSOM*. ABOVE: LANDING AT BOUNTY BAY TODAY IS STILL VERY HAZARDOUS BECAUSE OF LARGE WAVES AND LACK OF A NATURAL HARBOR.

BELOW: THE *PANDORA* WAS WRECKED ON A REEF BY THE NEGLIGENT CAPTAIN EDWARDS WHO IMPRISONED THE REMAINING *BOUNTY* SAILORS HE FOUND ON TAHITI SERVING AS MERCENARIES FOR TRIBAL WARS. THE *BOUNTY*'S FIREARMS CHANGED THE RULING POWERS OF TAHITI.

"Well, she is my aunt, and my cousin too. And also my step-sister, my niece, my fourth cousin, my thirty-third cousin, my forty-second cousin, my great aunt, my grandmother, my widowed sister-in-law—and next week she will be my wife."

With palm trees, lemon, banyan, and banana Pitcairn is more lush than one might imagine. Flowers are everywhere, including hibiscus, oleanders and frangipani. With its jagged cliffs the island is reminiscent of the Marquesas.

In Bounty Bay, where the mutineers' ship was stripped of her contents, run aground, and burned, divers today swim over the "Bones of the Bounty." Many relics have been found, including a cannon and the anchor which is mounted in the town square.

The Pitcairn people are clean, orderly, healthy, and cheerful. A couple of houses have washing machines, freezers, and video T.V., purchased with profits from the island's main industry—stamps. The plates are changed often, making them collectors' items for philatelists all over the world. Pitcairn's revenue is about one million dollars a year.

Whenever a ship leaves Pitcairn, the islanders sing their heartfelt song. Sterling Hayden, the late actor, sailor, and author, said, "When you hear the Pitcairners sing their goodbye songs everyone cries."

"In the sweet bye and bye,
 In the beautiful land beyond the sky . . .
 We shall part, never more when we meet
 On the be-yoo-tee-fool shore . . ."

Some people believe that Fletcher Christian actually escaped from the island on a passing whaling ship because no grave of the island's founder has been discovered, nor has even one gold coin been found of the *Bounty* treasure, which was carried in the cash box that all ships of the time maintained for expenditures on long voyages.

Peter Heywood, Christian's best friend on the *Bounty*, who declined to take part in the mutiny and had strongly urged Christian against it, swears he saw Christian on the streets of London some years later. After he called out "Fletcher," the man turned; Heywood got a good look at him, and then the man abruptly fled down an alleyway.

The Rime of the Ancient Mariner by Coleridge is said to be based on the story of the *Bounty*. In his private journals at the time of writing the poem, Coleridge makes several notes that some scholars assume refer to clandestine visits with Fletcher Christian in England.

BELOW: THE FIRST PERSON TO BE BORN ON PITCAIRN, THURSDAY OCTOBER CHRISTIAN, WEARING A PLUMED HAT.

THURSDAY OCTOBER CHRISTIAN AS AN OLD MAN. HE DIED ON TAHITI WHEN THE PITCAIRNERS UNSUCCESSFULLY ATTEMPTED TO SETTLE THERE BECAUSE OF OVERCROWDING ON THEIR OWN ISLAND.

ANDREW YOUNG, THE BEARDED PATRIARCH, REVEALED MUCH OF PITCAIRN'S ORAL HISTORY AS HE KNEW THURSDAY OCTOBER CHRISTIAN II (FLETCHER'S GRANDSON), WHO KNEW MAMATUA, FLETCHER'S WIFE, WHO TOLD HIM THE STORIES OF THE ISLAND'S SETTLEMENT AND THE HORRENDOUS MURDERS. ANDREW DIED JUST A FEW YEARS AGO, AT 89 YEARS OLD, SEVERING THE LAST LINK OF PITCAIRN'S RICH HISTORY.

It will very naturally be asked, what could be the reason for such a revolt? In answer to which I can only conjecture, that the mutineers had flattered themselves with the hopes of a more happy life among the Otaheiteans than they could possibly enjoy in England; and this, joined to some female connexions, most probably occasioned the whole transaction.

~ WILLIAM BLIGH, NARRATIVE OF THE VOYAGE
OF THE BOUNTY TO OTAHEITE

LEFT: A REPLICA OF
THE H.M.S. BOUNTY.
THE BOUNTY HAS
BEEN THE SUBJECT OF
FOUR MAJOR FILMS
AND MORE THAN
2,500 BOOKS AND
ARTICLES. RIGHT:
STAMPS FROM
PITCAIRN ISLANDS
PROVIDE MOST OF THE
PITCAIRNERS'
REVENUE.

ABOVE: BLIGH AND
NINETEEN MEN BEING
SET ADRIFT IN THE
BOUNTY'S TWENTY-
THREE-FEET LAUNCH.
BLIGH IS IN HIS NIGHT
SHIRT BECAUSE THE
MUTINEERS HAD
AWAKENED HIM IN THE
EARLY HOURS OF THE
MORNING. THE
MUTINEERS REFUSED
TO PROVIDE THE
CUSTOMARY MUSKETS,
BUT TO THE MEN IN
THE BOAT THEY THREW
IN FOUR CUTLASSES.
DURING THE
REMARKABLE 3,816-
MILE VOYAGE TO
TIMOR, ONLY ONE
MAN DIED — STONED
TO DEATH BY THE
NATIVES OF TONGA
WHEN THE SAILORS
LANDED FOR
PROVISIONS.

The ship drove fast, loud roared
    the blast,
And southward aye we fled.

And I had done a hellish thing,
And it would work 'em woe:

Day after day, day after day,
We stuck, nor breath nor motion;

Water, water, every where,
Nor any drop to drink.

Alone on a wide wide sea!
And never a saint took pity on
My soul in agony.

~SAMUEL TAYLOR COLERIDGE,
THE RIME OF THE ANCIENT MARINER

DEAN CHRISTIAN,
A DIRECT
DESCENDENT OF THE
MUTINEER, IN
"CHRISTIAN'S
CAVE." FLETCHER
CHRISTIAN WOULD
OFTEN GO TO A
CAVE HIGH ON THE
HILL AND BROOD
OVER HIS
MISFORTUNE AT
BEING ISOLATED ON
THE ISLAND.
FLETCHER CAME
FROM AN
ARISTOCRATIC
FAMILY IN
CUMBERLAND,
ENGLAND, AND
HAD GONE TO
SCHOOL WITH
WILLIAM
WORDSWORTH.
OPPOSITE PAGE:
GUSTAVE DORE'S
ILLUSTRATION FOR
*RIME OF THE
ANCIENT MARINER*
BY COLERIDGE,
WHO WAS INSPIRED
BY THE MUTINY ON
THE *BOUNTY* TO
WRITE THE EPIC
POEM.

PITCAIRN AVENUE, ADAMSTOWN, PITCAIRN, IN 1894. AN OCCASIONAL SHIPWRECKED SAILOR ADDED TO THE ISLAND'S POPULATION; HOWEVER, THE PITCAIRNERS REMAIN PREDOMINANTLY CHILDREN OF THE MUTINEERS.

DOWNTOWN ADAMSTOWN, IN 1894. TO THIS DAY, PITCAIRNERS SPEAK A DIALECT INCOMPREHENSIBLE TO ENGLISH OR POLYNESIANS; HOWEVER, THEY CAN ALSO SPEAK GOOD ENGLISH WITH A PECULIAR ACCENT TO VISITORS.

AN ISLAND TWO MILES LONG AND ONE MILE WIDE HAS CAPTURED THE IMAGINATION FOR OVER 200 YEARS. WHERE IS THE GRAVE OF FLETCHER CHRISTIAN AND THE GOLD FROM THE *BOUNTY*? SEVERAL PEOPLE, INCLUDING A *BOUNTY* SAILOR, PETER HEYWOOD, CLAIMED TO HAVE SEEN FLETCHER IN ENGLAND. IS IT POSSIBLE THAT CHRISTIAN WAS ONLY WOUNDED DURING THE MASSACRES, HID OUT IN HIS CAVE, ESCAPED IN THE *BOUNTY*'S CUTTER, AND WAS PICKED UP BY A WHALING SHIP? THE MYSTERY REMAINS.

THE LANDING AT BOUNTY BAY WHERE THE *BOUNTY* WAS RUN AGROUND, STRIPPED, AND BURNED BY THE MUTINEERS.

INBREEDING AMONGST PITCAIRNERS HAS HAD FEW NEGATIVE EFFECTS, SINCE THEY STARTED WITH HEALTHY STOCK ON BOTH THE ENGLISH AND TAHITIAN SIDES.

IN THE EARLY 1800S, THE PITCAIRN WOMEN BORE AN AVERAGE OF ELEVEN CHILDREN PER WOMAN. MARIA CHRISTIAN, BORN IN 1815, MARRIED AT FOURTEEN YEARS OLD, PRODUCED TWENTY-FIVE CHILDREN, AND SURVIVED THREE HUSBANDS! SUCH ARE THE PITCAIRN GENES.

LEFT: PITCAIRN WAS INDEED A FRAGILE PARADISE. AFTER FOUR YEARS, THE TAHITIAN MEN AND THE ENGLISH HAD KILLED EACH OTHER. EVENTUALLY, THE SOLE SURVIVING ADULT MALE, JOHN ADAMS, LIVED PROMISCUOUSLY FOR MANY YEARS WITH THE REMAINING NINE TAHITIAN WOMEN AND TOOK CARE OF THE TWENTY-FIVE CHILDREN.

TWELVE TAHITIAN WOMEN AND SIX MEN ACCOMPANIED THE MUTINEERS TO BECOME SELF-IMPOSED CASTAWAYS ON PITCAIRN.

RIGHT: A SINK ON THE PORCH OF A PITCAIRN HOUSE EMBODIES THE SIMPLICITY OF THE PITCAIRN LIFE, FAR REMOVED FROM THE MODERN WORLD.

BELOW LEFT: A PRAYER WRITTEN BY JOHN ADAMS. AFTER THE MASSACRES, HE BECAME VERY RELIGIOUS AND TAUGHT THE CHILDREN WITH THE *BOUNTY* BIBLE. ADAMS' REAL NAME WAS ALEXANDER SMITH. HE LIED ABOUT BEING INNOCENT IN THE MUTINY, CHANGED HIS STORY OF CHRISTIAN'S DEATH AT LEAST THREE TIMES, AND ADMITTED TO MURDERING MATTHEW QUINTAL. HOWEVER, HE CONVINCED ALL VISITORS OF HIS TOTAL REDEMPTION.

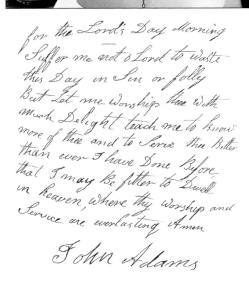

for the Lord's Day Morning
Suffer me not o Lord to waste this Day in Sin or folly But Let me worship thee with much Delight teach me to know more of thee and to Serve thee Better than ever I have Done Before, that I may Be fitter to Dwell in heaven, where thy worship and Service are everlasting Amen

John Adams

RIGHT: THE ORIGINAL *BOUNTY* BIBLE WHICH IS KEPT UNDER GLASS IN THE CHURCH ON PITCAIRN ISLAND. IT TAKES THREE KEYS HELD BY THREE DIFFERENT RESPONSIBLE PITCAIRNERS TO UNLOCK THE CASE TO VIEW THE BIBLE.

The Mutineer

Bible

of 1789

Presented by

John Adams grand son

of the Patriarch of Pitcairn

Island to Sir Hayden

_____ 1889 and held

by Rebekiah Smith President

of the American Seaman's

Society. _____ York from 1881

and at this date given in charge

of DC Sydney Hayden

of Windsor

Sir Hayden

jan 30

RED-FOOTED, BROWN, AND MASKED BOOBIES ON UNINHABITED DUCIE ISLAND, ONE OF THE PITCAIRN GROUP. BOOBIES NEST IN COLONIES AND OFTEN CONGREGATE IN THOUSANDS ON THEIR ISLANDS. THEY FLY HIGHER THAN MOST SEABIRDS AND ARE OFTEN ATTRACTED TO SHIPS.

RED-TAILED
TROPICBIRD. THE RED
FEATHERS FROM THESE
BIRDS ARE VALUED AS
ORNAMENTS ON MANY
POLYNESIAN ISLANDS.

The Pacific is inconstant and
uncertain like the soul of man....
 You sail through an unimag-
inable silence upon a magic sea.
Now and then a few gulls
suggest that land is not far off,
a forgotten island hidden in a
wilderness of waters; but the
gulls, the melancholy gulls, are
the only sign you have of it.

~ W. SOMERSET MAUGHAM,
THE TREMBLING OF A LEAF, 1921

LEFT: ONE OF THE
NUMEROUS TERNS ON
DUCIE, A BIRDS'
PARADISE. *RIGHT:*
FRIGATE BIRDS AND
BABY FRIGATE.

MANGAREVA THE FORGOT~ TEN ISLANDS

NCE CALLED THE GAMBIER ISLANDS, MANGAREVA, as it was known in ancient times and again today, consists of eight small, high islands, 1,000 miles southeast of Tahiti. It is the closest landfall from Pitcairn. Mangareva, the main island, once famous for large natural pearls, today has cultured pearl farms that are among the finest in French Polynesia.

The first thing one notices on the island are the many churches, old stone buildings, and arches resembling ruins of a Spanish town. These are reminders of a religious fanatic—Père Laval—the mad priest who made Mangareva the center for Catholic missions in Polynesia.

In the nineteenth century, a whaling ship first brought stories of the islands to Valparaiso, Chile, where Laval served as a priest in the monastery of the Jesuit Order of Picpus. He was intrigued by tales of a cannibal king and pearls, which the people valued so lightly they exchanged them with sailors for mere trinkets.

Laval was ambitious to do something not only for the church, but for his own glory, driven in his ambition by a deadly fanaticism. In 1834, Laval, with one other priest, arrived in Rikitea. He eventually won the confidence of the last king of the island, Maputeoa, by promising him palaces, towers, and courts such as those owned by the magnificent kings of Europe. Once in control, the priest then set the

DUST JACKET COVER FOR *MANGAREVA* BY ROBERT LEE ESKRIDGE, 1931. THE AUTHOR DESCRIBES LIFE ON THE ISLAND, MYSTICISM, AND *TUPAPA'U* (GHOSTS), WHICH THE NATIVES CLAIM ARE THE

PHANTOMS OF THE NIGHT. HE WENT THERE TO PAINT AND WRITE IN 1929 AFTER THE STOCK MARKET CRASH, EVENTUALLY SETTLING IN HAWAII. *ABOVE:* PAINTINGS BY ESKRIDGE, A CLASSICIST, WHO

TURNED MODERNIST UNDER THE INFLUENCE OF HIS PEERS, MARK TOBY AND GEORGIA O'KEEFE. HIS PAINTINGS, COLLECTED BY EDWARD G. ROBINSON, HUNG

ON THE WALLS NEXT TO GAUGUIN'S AT MCCORMICK'S MANSION IN CHICAGO. UNLIKE GAUGUIN, ESKRIDGE IS NOW FORGOTTEN— LIKE THE ISLANDS HE PAINTED.

entire population to work, cutting blocks of coral to make his empire.

The Polynesians, unused to long, continuous work, died under the hard labor. When Maputeoa pleaded for Laval to have mercy on the people, the priest answered, "Make them work day and night! Only by such righteous labor can they expiate the sins of their lustful ancestors!"

Why did they accept this foreigner's religion and not revolt, kill and eat him? The answer lies not in the Catholic religion but in the islanders' own culture. Ancient prophecies foretold the day when two men would arrive, bringing with them a god greater than their own gods. With Laval, they believed that the prophecy had been fulfilled; they agreed to destroy their temples and knock down statues depicting the ancient deities because this new god was all powerful.

Rumors of Laval's autocratic rule and his accumulation of a fortune in pearls circulated throughout Papeete. In 1864, Comte Emile de La Roncière, the new governor of Tahiti, visited the Gambiers with full authority from the French government, thus ending Laval's mad annihilation of the natives.

The governor asked Laval, "What sort of government do you call this? Five thousand men and boys dead in ten years, over half the population, from this mad building plan of yours!"

Laval then made his famous defense. "True, monsieur Le Comte, they are dead, but they have gone to heaven the more quickly!"

ESKRIDGE TALKING
WITH EMILE, THE SON
OF PAUL GAUGUIN.
YEARS LATER, IN
1962, A WOMAN TOOK
EMILE TO CHICAGO
TO STUDY ART. AFTER
EXHIBITIONS IN
LONDON, PARIS, AND
NEW YORK, IT WAS
REALIZED HE HAD NO
TALENT IN ART; HE
RETURNED TO A BASIC
LIFE IN TAHITI.

SCENES OF
MANGAREVA AND THE
ASTROLABE OF
DUMONT D'URVILLE'S
EXPEDITION
ANCHORED OFF
RIKITEA.

*Natives
seen here*

G

D

C

B

GAMBIER's ISLANDS

CHART OF THE
GAMBIER ISLANDS
(MANGAREVA) DRAWN
DURING CAPTAIN
COOK'S VOYAGE.

There are certain parts of the
world—like our American
mountains, deserts, and lonely
stretches of coast—which seem
planned for the spiritual refresh-
ment of mankind; places from
which one carries away a new
serenity and the sense of a
yearning for beauty satisfied.
Ever since the days of Cook the
islands of the South Sea have
charmed the white man—
explorers, naturalists, traders,
and the rough crews of whaling
vessels; the strange beauty of
these little lands, insignificant so
far as commercial exploitation is
concerned, seems worthy of
preservation.

~ JAMES NORMAN HALL AND
CHARLES NORDHOFF,
FAERY LANDS OF THE SOUTH SEAS

ACCOMPLISHED
SEAMEN, THE ANCIENT
POLYNESIANS USED
CELESTIAL
NAVIGATION TO
TRAVEL GREAT
DISTANCES. WILLIAM
SMYTH DREW THESE
MANGAREVANS IN
THEIR DOUBLE-
HULLED CANOE
DURING BEECHEY'S
VOYAGE OF 1825-28.

RIGHT: THIS ISLAND
FAMILY USES A SPEED-
BOAT TO GET SUPPLIES
IN RIKITEA, THE
SMALL TOWN ON
MANGAREVA. THE
TIHONI REASIN
FAMILY, OF AMERICAN
AND TAHITIAN
DESCENT, LIVES A
ROBINSON CRUSOE
STYLE OF LIFE ON
KAMAKA, THEIR
PRIVATE ISLAND, SEEN
IN THE BACKGROUND
OF THIS PICTURE.

Above: The first
schoolhouse and
a fallen *tiki*
(statue) in
Mangareva in the
1800s.

Right: Children
in school in
Mangareva. The
French government
provides an
excellent
educational system
throughout
French Polynesia.

Below: The first
encounters between
the Europeans and
the natives
frequently were not
of the friendliest
nature.

At this moment Mr. Morgan appeared barefooted on the porch of his new house. Behind him stood the girl Maeva, her face bandaged. With long, careless steps, his toes kicking dust, the stranger walked along the dusty road and right up to the line of wardens. "Which one of them was it, Maeva?"

The handsome girl, her hair down to her waist, stepped from behind Mr. Morgan and pointed fearlessly at one of the worst wardens. "That one," she said.

The white man lifted his shotgun and there was a terrified gasp from the crowd, but he handed it to the girl and said, "I showed you how to use this. If anyone—a warden, the pastor, anyone comes at me, kill him."

Then slowly, like a wave about to crash upon the reef, he went to the warden who had beaten Maeva and with a sudden grab pulled the hulking man out of line. In silence, and in fearful efficiency, he beat the man until it seemed as if his small right hand could drive no more. The warden was fat, cowardly. Twice Mr. Morgan hauled him to his feet and waited until the bully got set. Then with merciless blows he knocked him down again. Blood was spattered across the white uniform.

MR. MORGAN WAS BASED ON THE STORY OF PÈRE LAVAL AND MANGAREVA ~ JAMES MICHENER, *RETURN TO PARADISE*

The island of tranquil delights
rose out of the sea a pyramid of
flowers girdled with a silver
zone; the reef that flashed and
sang, opened to admit us,
and then seemed to close again
and shut us in a little world
of unutterable beauty.

~ CHARLES WARREN STODDARD,
THE ISLAND OF TRANQUIL DELIGHTS, 1873

MANGAREVA AT
SUNSET, VIEWED
FROM THE LOVELY
ISLET AUKENA.

COOK ISLANDS LONELY ISLANDS

THE NEXT ISLANDS WEST OF THE AUSTRALS ARE THE Cook Islands, lying about 700 miles southwest of Tahiti. The Cooks have been independent since 1965 but are a British Protectorate administered by New Zealand; consequently, the people on the islands speak English.

Rarotonga, the main island, resembles Tahiti of twenty-five years ago, easy going and slow-paced. The Arorangi prison there is unique: Where else could you find inmates playing lawn tennis, volley ball, and producing the island's best ukuleles? Tennis tournaments are the highlight of prison life.

According to the tender-hearted chief warden, most of the prisoners are harmless, but the sentences are harsh. Many offenders have been deported from New Zealand. In the prison they get three meals a day, and for most this is better than they were accustomed to on the outside. On Saturdays, the well-behaved married prisoners are allowed to return home to their wives. They don't escape, since there is nowhere to run to.

The prison is situated in a fertile valley, surrounded by banana plantations and vegetable gardens. Prisoners not only grow their own produce but also supply the island with fresh food. Some of the younger inmates are hired out during the day to families to work on farms.

Not all the inmates are petty thieves. As friendly as Polynesians are, they are also hot blooded, macho, and jealous. Fist fights and wife beating are common, and there are more rapes per capita in Polynesia than in most countries.

Alcohol is a problem for most Polynesians. The usual explanation is that their bodies cannot metabolize alcohol quickly because of a deficiency in their livers. *Kava*, on the other hand, is a traditional Polynesian drink that they handle better. Although it does not contain alcohol, it is intoxicating. Made from roots, *kava* was frequently used for religious ceremonies and as a daily beverage. It is still used today on many islands throughout the South Pacific, but less frequently in

KOTZEBUE, RUSSIAN EXPLORER, LANDING ON PENRHYN ISLAND IN 1816, DRAWN BY THE GIFTED YOUNG PAINTER LOUIS CHORIS. (PENRHYN WAS NAMED AFTER THE FIRST SHIP TO VISIT THERE, *LADY PENRHYN*, AN ENGLISH SHIP IN 1788.) TEN YEARS EARLIER THAN KOTZEBUE, ANOTHER RUSSIAN, VON KRUSENSTERN, VISITED THESE ISLANDS. HE CHANGED THEIR NAME FROM THE HERVEY ISLANDS, AS CAPTAIN COOK HAD CALLED THEM, TO THE COOK ISLANDS.

French territories or the Cooks where it is now illegal.

The outer islands are still unspoiled. A favorite of visitors is Aitutaki Island, 141 miles north of Rarotonga. An interesting marriage of an island and an atoll, Aitutaki Island has a triangular shaped lagoon with many atolls sprinkled throughout. The main island is raised but not mountainous like Bora Bora or Rarotonga. What is unique about Aitutaki are the shifting colors of blue in the lagoon. Ranging from pale turquoise to deep ultramarine, this intriguing effect is caused by light reflecting off suspended grains of sand in the water.

Farther north from Aitutaki is Palmerston, which was first settled in 1863, by an Englishman named William Marsters. With three Polynesian wives, he started his own island domain and refused to allow any other men to settle there. Today, there are nearly 5,000 people on the island, all descendents of William Marsters.

The next island from Palmerston is Puka Puka, where Robert Dean Frisbie lived in 1924 and wrote his romantic South Pacific books. Michener described Frisbie as "the most graceful poetic and sensitive writer ever to have reported on the islands." Here is what Frisbie wrote about the lonely Northern Cook Islands: *"Everything is dreamlike here. The island itself is a dream come true, so that romanticists who are patient enough and adventurous enough may see vindicated their faith in lonely lands beyond the farthest horizons."*

If Puka Puka is not remote enough, there is uninhabited Suwarrow, 513 miles north of Rarotonga, made famous in *An Island to Myself* by Tom Neale. Neale wrote: *"I chose to live in the Pacific islands because life there moves at the sort of pace which you feel God must have had in mind originally when He made the sun to keep us warm and provided the fruits of the earth for the taking."*

To live alone on an island, one must be truly adventurous and a tropical survivor, excelling at fishing, farming, and being a jack-of-all-trades. Tom Neale survived quite happily alone for five years, unlike some previous inhabitants of Suwarrow: During World War II, a seaplane was forced to land at the island. Only the skeletal remains of the seven castaways were found. With coconuts and fish all around them, they starved to death not knowing the basics of island living.

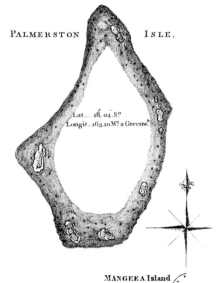

PALMERSTON ISLE.

Lat. 18.04.S°
Longit. 163.10.W! a Greenw.

MANGEEA Island
Lat. 21.57.S.
Long. 201.53.E.

ABOVE: A VERY ROMANTIC VERSION OF PARADISE, PAINTED BY ROBERT MEYERS IN THE 1950s, ILLUSTRATES WILLIAM MARSTERS AND HIS THREE WIVES WHO STARTED THEIR OWN ISLAND DOMAIN ON PALMERSTON DURING THE MID-1800s. MIDDLE AND RIGHT: CAPTAIN COOK MADE INCREDIBLY ACCURATE CHARTS THROUGHOUT POLYNESIA.

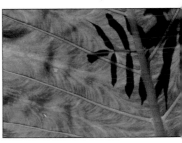

ABOVE: TROPICAL PALM ON RAROTONGA. *LEFT:* GIRL WEARING A PALM-FROND HAT, MADE IN MINUTES ON ONE OF THE MANY *MOTU* (ISLETS) OF AITUTAKI.

SIR ALBERT HENRY'S
GRANDSON, OF
AITUTAKI, SPEARED A
JACK TREVALLY IN
THE TRADITIONAL
METHOD—FROM THE
BEACH. IT IS ALSO A
FAVORITE FISH OF
LIGHT TACKLE
ANGLERS.

WOMAN FANNING
HERSELF IN CHURCH.
MOST POLYNESIANS
ARE PROTESTANT AND
ATTEND CHURCH
REGULARLY.

In short the more one is acquainted with these people the better one likes them, to give them their due I must say they are the most obliging and benevolent people I ever met with.

~ CAPTAIN JAMES COOK,
JOURNAL, SEPTEMBER 1773

ABOVE: SHADOW OF AN AIRPLANE FLYING OVER ONE OF THE MANY BARRIER REEFS.
RIGHT: PORTRAIT OF CAPTAIN JAMES COOK.

STATUE OF SIR ALBERT HENRY ON RAROTONGA. HE WAS THE FIRST PRIME MINISTER OF THE COOK ISLANDS BUT WAS REMOVED FROM OFFICE FOR BALLOT STUFFING. THE SPECTACLES ON THE STATUE ARE HIS VERY OWN.

PAHUA (DELICIOUS EDIBLE CLAMS FOUND ON THE REEFS).

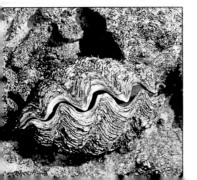

An island attracts one strangely and inexplicably. In our youngest days few pleasures have been so great as exploring some tiny bank formed by the forking of a stream, or of dreaming that some day we shall sail to an island in the

> …moonlit solitudes mild
> Of the mid-most ocean….

And as we grow older the fascination is not lost. Any man with a spark of poetry in his soul will stand on the deck of a ship to stare, captivated, at an island, while a mainland, even though it be more beautiful, will command but a passing glance.

~ ROBERT DEAN FRISBIE, *MY TAHITI*, 1924

ROBERT DEAN FRISBIE AND HIS YOUNG WIFE FROM PUKA PUKA. MICHENER DESCRIBED FRISBIE AS, "THE MOST GRACEFUL, POETIC, AND SENSITIVE WRITER EVER TO HAVE REPORTED ON THE ISLANDS."

COMING IN THROUGH THE NARROW PASS IN THE REEF AFTER FISHING THE TURBULENT WATERS OFF AITUTAKI. DEEP SEA FISHING IS EXCELLENT THROUGHOUT POLYNESIA FOR MARLIN, TUNA, BONITO, BARRACUDA, AND *MAHI MAHI*.

SIGN DEPICTING HOW REMOTE AITUTAKI IS FROM THE REST OF THE WORLD.

ABOVE: A TYPICAL ISLAND STORE AND MAIN STREET AITUTAKI.
RIGHT: YOUNG GIRLS RETURNING FROM CHURCH.

I threw one look to either hand,
And I knew I was in Fairyland.

~ ROBERT LOUIS STEVENSON

BELOW TOP: A GIRL CARRYING HOME THE DAILY BREAD FLAVORED WITH COCONUT. *BELOW BOTTOM:* DOMESTIC PIGS FREQUENTLY CAN BE FOUND IN THE COOK ISLANDERS' YARDS AS IN THIS PHOTO TAKEN ON RAROTONGA.

…news of highest consequence
I miss; and feast of wit and flow of soul.
I do not care. Mid-ocean solitudes
Offer as of old, a recompense…"

~ James Norman Hall

EASTER ISLAND
RAPA NUI

HROUGHOUT POLYNESIA THERE WERE PERSISTENT traditions to the effect that another people had been living on the islands when the ancestors of the present population arrived. Everywhere within the Polynesian triangle, which extends from Easter Island in the east to Samoa and New Zealand in the west and to Hawaii in the north, the learned men of the tribes agreed: an industrious people with reddish hair and fair skin, claiming descent from the sun god, were found on the various islands and were expelled or absorbed by the newcomers.

~THOR HEYERDAHL, *FATU-HIVA, BACK TO NATURE*

Easter Island has captured the world's imagination with its enormous statues (some 600 are on the island), which are unlike any other statues found in the Pacific. The island, 2,300 miles west of Chile and 2,600 miles east of Tahiti, is completely isolated from other civilizations.

But how did people arrive on this remote island in the first place?

EASTER ISLANDERS
PADDLING AN
OUTRIGGER CANOE
DURING THE
EIGHTEENTH
CENTURY.

IF THE *RONGO-RONGO*
(WOOD WRITING
TABLETS) COULD BE
DECIPHERED, THEY
MIGHT SOLVE THE
MYSTERIES.

Most anthropologists agree that the people of Rapa Nui, like most Polynesians, migrated originally from Indonesia in large sailing canoes about 400-500 A.D. But Thor Heyerdahl, author of *Kon-Tiki, Aku-Aku,* and several other books on Polynesia, believes that the Easter Islanders and the Marquesans arrived on rafts built of reeds from South America. His theories are controversial; most anthropologists and archeologists disagree with his conclusions. Recent mitochondrial DNA tests of Easter Island skeletons proved identical to mitochondrial DNA tests from living Polynesians and ancient Polynesian skeletons, which proves that the Easter Islanders are of Polynesian origin. No DNA tests have been found to be identical to Peruvian or Chilean ancestry.

The statues themselves were made with stone picks of hard basalt, which were left by the thousands in the quarries. Between 1200 and 1500 A.D., the Easter Islanders carved the statues in the mountain at the crater Rano Raraku, transported them with the use of timber down to the coast, and set them upon altars with the help of piled stones. The island today is almost entirely deforested, making the statues even more monolithic and singular.

The statues commemorated ancestors whose *mana* (power) brought benefit to the community. The people who built the statues were not slaves, but artists, who believed they would attain supernatural powers.

Tablets of wood carved with hieroglyphics, called *rongo-rongo,* proved that Easter Island had a society much more complicated than other Polynesian islands where no writing has been found.

The building of the statues reached a climax, then suddenly stopped;

ABOVE LEFT: ONE OF THE OLDEST STATUES ON THE ISLAND IS DIFFERENT FROM THE OTHERS: THE FIGURE KNEELS AND SPORTS A GOATEE. *ABOVE RIGHT:* CHRISTIANITY REPLACED THE ISLAND'S BIRD-MAN CULT. PAGAN BIRD-MAN FIGURES ADORN THE PEDESTIAL BELOW A STATUE OF JESUS CHRIST. *ABOVE:* A NECKLACE MADE OF SHELLS FROM THE WATERS WHICH SURROUND EASTER ISLAND.

  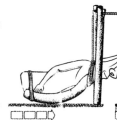  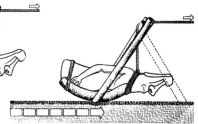

DURING EXCAVATIONS ON EASTER ISLAND, SONIA HAOA, A NATIVE EASTER ISLAND ARCHEOLOGIST, WAS CREDITED WITH FINDING MANY SCULPTURED EYES THAT HAD BEEN MISSING ON THE STATUES. HERE SHE PLACES THE *MATA* (EYES) BACK ON ONE OF THE STATUES. ORIGINALLY, SOME OF THE STATUES WERE CARVED WITH EYES SO THAT THEY COULD LOOK OVER THE PEOPLE AND GUIDE THEM WITH THEIR *MANA* (SUPERNATURAL POWER).

the islanders left their tools and many of the statues half-finished. By the time the first European explorers arrived, they found the people living in a state of anarchy amidst the ruins. The first discoverer was Jacob Roggeveen, a Dutchman who arrived on Easter Day in 1722, hence the name, Easter Island. Captain Cook, when visiting the island in 1774, called the stone statues "Monuments of Antiquity" and noted that the inhabitants did not even repair them.

According to legend, a civil war broke out between the *Hanau eepe* (the Long-ears) a group who arrived later on the island, and the *Hanau momoko* (the Short-ears) who battled them for supremacy. After the wars and the abandonment of the statues, the culture collapsed; violence and cannibalism followed. The people then destroyed the Ahus and toppled the statues.

John Dos Passos, who visited in 1969, saw the Easter Island tragedy as less an isolated enigma than as a dangerous cycle happening in "civilized" society as well.

Setting up great statues might not seem important to present-day Americans but to these people it must have been the be-all and the end-all.

Then suddenly, so far as we know without any foreign invasion, all this energy was turned towards destruction.

… Twenty years ago, even ten years ago, the Easter Island story wouldn't have seemed so cogent to an American. We were still hopefully committed to the building of a civilization. It never occurred to us that we were breeding a generation of wreckers. Great blocks of steel and glass skyscrapers full of the whir of typewriters and people pushing papers back and forth across desks probably wouldn't have seemed any more important to an Easter Islander than their weird statues seem to us, but we see them as part of a complicated social structure which assures food, clothing and shelter and an incredible number of amenities to many millions of people. Today, again without any massive impulse from the outside, counterparts have appeared in our society of the wreckers who had themselves a time pulling down the silly old statues on Easter Island. "None of it is any good, let's make an end of it."

Probably it didn't occur to the Easter Island revolutionists any more than it does to our college radicals that their own food and shelter depended on the social order they were pulling down. Undoubtedly agitators told them that if they overthrew the statues the oppression of

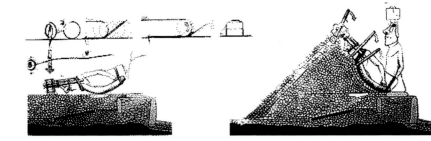

the Longears would fall with them. Justice and plenty would reign. Nobody would have to work any more. The result was a hundred years of arson and famine and murder and the near extinction of a talented and effective community.

JOHN DOS PASSOS, *EASTER ISLAND, ISLAND OF ENIGMAS*

A new group or cult called the *Tangata Manu* or "Bird-man" appeared. Each year in September, they held their sacred ceremonies dedicated to the *Manutara* (Sooty Tern) at Orongo, a site on the rim of the crater Rano Kau. The birds were considered reincarnations of spirits. At the ceremonies, a man from each clan was chosen to climb down the steep cliffs, then swim through the strong currents and waves to the small *tapu* islands off the tip of Easter Island. The first man to find a seabird egg shouted out the name of his chief and swam back with the egg. He was considered *tapu*, possessor of supernatural powers, for the rest of the year.

Today, at Anakena, is found the only coconut grove on the entire island. The coconuts had been brought from Tahiti by the Chilean navy aboard the *Esmeralda*, a great sailing ship in 1960. Originally, there were more coconuts; however, many of those planted in the main village were dug up and eaten by the islanders. Because Easter Island produces little food, most food is flown in from Chile and sold at a high prices. How do the islanders survive? On a very fragile economic thread. Half of the workers are employed by the Chilean government for the island's and the National Park's upkeep. Others fish, farm and guide tourists who come to see the statues. The people help one another out, because family ties and a sense of community are very strong on the island.

A MAP OF EASTER ISLAND WHICH WAS CHARTED BY CAPTAIN COOK. THE NATIVES CALLED THEIR ISLAND *TE-PITO-O-TE-HENUA* (THE NAVEL-OF-THE-WORLD).

TOURISM IS HELPING THE ISLAND'S ECONOMY. EASTER ISLAND HAS ABOUT 4,000 VISITORS ANNUALLY. *ABOVE:* A PLANE FLIES OVER THE WORLD'S MOST INTRIGUING OUTDOOR SCULPTURE GARDEN IN THE DISTRICT OF ANAKENA. BY THE TIME CAPTAIN COOK ARRIVED, MANY OF THE STATUES HAD ALREADY BEEN TOPPLED OVER DURING TRIBAL WARS AND BY *TSUNAMIS* (GIANT PACIFIC TIDAL WAVES). AFTER THE NATIVES CUT DOWN MOST OF THE TREES TO TRANSPORT THE STATUES, THE ISLAND BECAME BARREN AND FAMINE RESULTED. WAR, ANARCHY, AND CANNIBALISM FOLLOWED.

...the crater of Rano Kao, the widest and possibly the most regularly shaped in the whole world. Seen from the sky it must give the effect that telescopes record on the moon…. The last king of Rapa Nui is supposed to have climbed up there to save himself and his people at the time of the Peruvian invasion and there the great massacre took place. The footpaths are full of bones and whole skeletons still appear half lost in the grass.

~ PIERRE LOTI, 1872

RIGHT: EASTER ISLAND MAN AND WOMAN, DRAWN BY LOUIS CHORIS IN 1816. THE *TOTORA* REEDS OF THE RAFT THE MAN IS HOLDING COME FROM THE CRATER (ABOVE). THE SAME TYPE OF REED AND REED RAFTS ARE FOUND IN PERU. IT IS LIKELY THAT THE ISLAND WAS PEOPLED BY POLYNESIANS *AND* SOUTH AMERICANS.

LEFT: DURING THE TRIBAL WARS, COMBATANTS BROKE THE STATUES' NECKS TO REDUCE THEIR POWER.

The ceremonial village of Orongo which you stumble on suddenly along the narrow footpath is one of the most romantic spots on the face of the earth. On one side is the deep cauldron of the crater, on the other the cliff. There's a dizzy sense of height…. There's an electric energy about the carving of the birdmen. In topsy-turvy juxtaposition you can make out a swarm of human figures with birds' heads, long hands raised in supplication.

~ JOHN DOS PASSOS,
EASTER ISLAND, ISLAND OF ENIGMAS

…while our attention was attracted by the women, we were robbed of our hats and handkerchiefs. They all appeared to be accomplices in the robbery; for scarcely was it accomplished, than like a flock of birds they all fled at the same instant; but seeing that we did not make use of our firelocks, they returned a few minutes after, recommended their caresses, and watched the moment for committing a new depredation…

~ LA PÉROUSE, 1786

ABOVE: ORONGO, WHERE THE BIRD-MEN HELD RELIGIOUS CEREMONIES. *BELOW:* COMTE JEAN-FRANÇOIS GALAUP DE LA PÉROUSE (1741-88) WAS SENT BY KING LOUIS XVI TO EXPLORE THE SOUTH SEAS.

LA PÉROUSE, THE FRENCH VERSION OF CAPTAIN COOK, HAD HIS ARTIST, DUCHÉ DE VANCY, DRAW THE FRENCH SAILORS ENAMORED WITH THE WOMEN OF EASTER ISLAND. MOST DRAWINGS WERE SENT BACK TO FRANCE BEFORE LA PÉROUSE WAS LOST AT SEA.

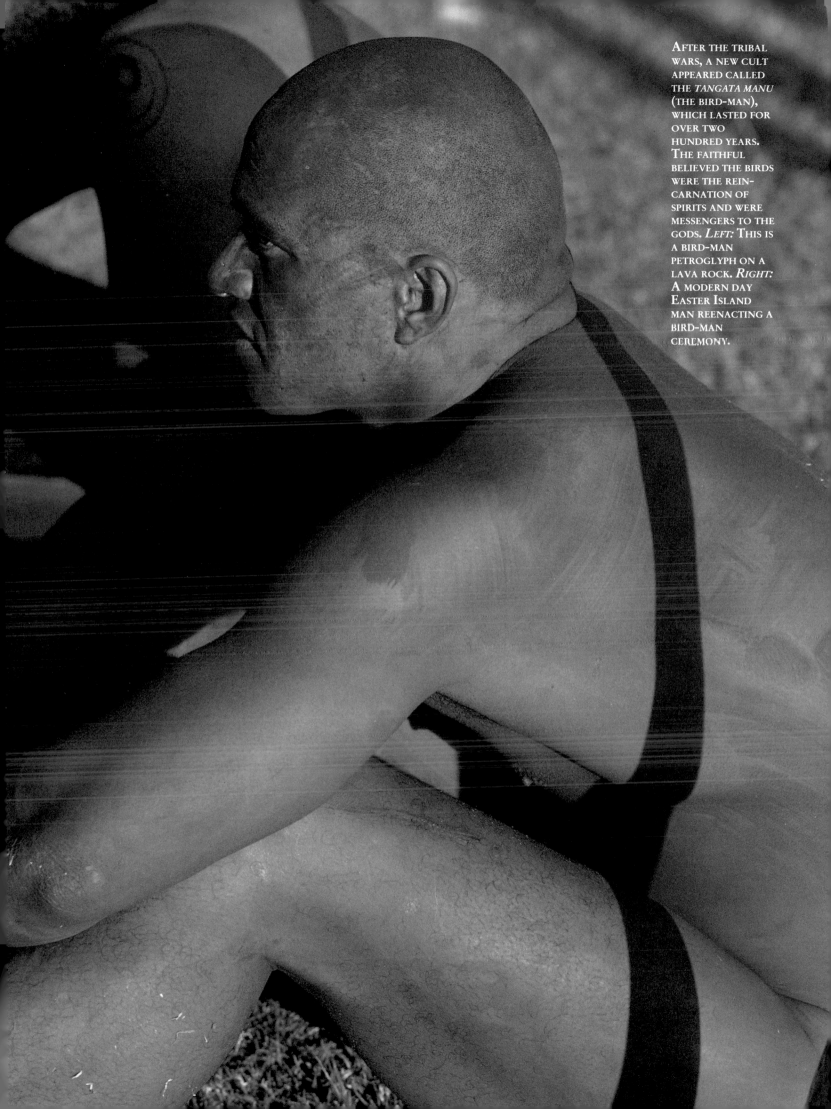

AFTER THE TRIBAL
WARS, A NEW CULT
APPEARED CALLED
THE *TANGATA MANU*
(THE BIRD-MAN),
WHICH LASTED FOR
OVER TWO
HUNDRED YEARS.
THE FAITHFUL
BELIEVED THE BIRDS
WERE THE REIN-
CARNATION OF
SPIRITS AND WERE
MESSENGERS TO THE
GODS. *LEFT:* THIS IS
A BIRD-MAN
PETROGLYPH ON A
LAVA ROCK. *RIGHT:*
A MODERN DAY
EASTER ISLAND
MAN REENACTING A
BIRD-MAN
CEREMONY.

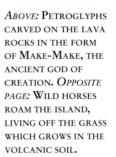

ANAKENA WAS THE LANDING PLACE OF THE FIRST CHIEF OF EASTER ISLAND, HOTU MATUA. THE EARLY EASTER ISLANDERS BROUGHT WITH THEM A COMPLEX RELIGION, SOCIAL STRUCTURE, AND FANTASTIC STONE-WORKING. THE STATUES HAVE ASTRONOMICAL SIGNIFICANCE: THEY ARE ALIGNED TO CHART THE MOVEMENT OF STARS, HELPING THE ISLANDERS TO TIME PLANTING, HARVESTING, AND CEREMONIAL EVENTS. SOME OF THE STATUES HAVE *PUKAO* (TOPKNOTS), REPRESENTING THE RED HAIR OF THE EARLY CHIEFS.

There exists in the midst of the great ocean, in a region where nobody goes, a mysterious and isolated island; no other land is near it and for more than eight hundred leagues in all directions empty and terrifying immensities surround it.

The island is planted with monstrous great statues, the work of I don't know what race, today degenerate or vanished; its great remains an enigma.

I went ashore there years ago in my green youth from a sailing frigate, after days of strong wind and obscuring clouds; there has remained with me the recollection of a half fantastic land, a land of dreams.

~ PIERRE LOTI, 1872

A STONE MAUSOLEUM.

TUAMOTUS THE DANGER~ OUS ISLANDS

OR THE MORE ADVENTUROUS, THERE IS THE Tuamotu Archipelago, known as the "Dangerous Islands" because countless ships have wrecked in this maze of seventy-six islands.

Atolls are volcanic islands, geologically much older than high volcanic islands. Atolls have sunk into the ocean over millions of years, leaving land on only the exposed rim of the crater, while the crater itself has become the lagoon. One of the largest atolls in the world is Rangiroa. For fishing, spear fishing, and scuba diving, the Rangiroa lagoon and pass is spectacular, but beware of the numerous sharks. In the Tuamotus, one occasionally sees a man who has lost an arm or a leg to a large shark while spear fishing. The most feared are the *mako* and especially the *mao tore tore*, the famous tiger shark. When a tiger shark is spotted, all spear fishing stops for up to two weeks on certain islands.

Some of the lagoons are scarcely more than salt-water ponds; others, like those of Rangiroa and Fakarava, are as much as fifty miles long by twenty or thirty across. The motu, or islets, composing the land, are threaded at wide intervals on the encircling reef. The smaller ones are frequented by sea fowl which nest in the pandanus trees and among the fronds of scattered coconut palms. Others, enchantingly green and restful to sea-weary eyes, follow the curve of the reef for many miles,

sloping away over the arc of the world until they are lost to view. But whatever their extent, one feature is common to all: they are mere fringes of land seldom more than a quarter of a mile in width, and rising only a few feet above the sea which seems always on the point of overwhelming them.

~ CHARLES NORDHOFF AND JAMES NORMAN HALL, *THE HURRICANE*

Fishing is one of the main industries. Most of the fish are caught in fish parks, chicken wire constructions which let the fish in, but prevent escape. The fish are easily speared, netted, refrigerated, and then sent to market in Papeete by plane or boat.

The Dangerous Islands boast a booming pearl industry, mainly on the islands of Manihi, Arutua, and Marutea. In the old days, the islanders used to dive for natural pearls. Overharvesting nearly destroyed the industry, but in 1963 Mikimoto introduced his Japanese pearl cultivation. The temperature and water conditions are ideal for the *Pinctada margaritifera*—black lipped pearl oyster, the only one to give birth to the true black pearl known worldwide. These pearls cost anywhere from $400 to $2,000 a piece, depending on size, shape, color, lustre, cleanliness of its surface, and quality of its deep inner glow, known as Orient.

Pearl farming is a profitable business for the truly adventurous, hard-working entrepreneur. It is also a gamble: it takes five years before any pearls are produced, and the crop can be ruined by disease, hurricanes, or pearl bandits. The oysters are strung on lines in about

TUAMOTU MAN WITH
A PADDLE, POSING IN
THE 1920S.

IN 1521, FERDINAND MAGELLAN WAS THE FIRST EUROPEAN TO CROSS THE PACIFIC, WHICH HE NAMED "MAR PACIFICO," AND THE FIRST TO SIGHT A POLYNESIAN ISLAND IN THE TUAMOTUS. HE CONTINUED ON TO THE PHILIPPINES TO CONVERT THE ISLANDERS TO CATHOLISM, BUT DIED OF WOUNDS FROM A POISON ARROW AND A JAVELIN IN THE LEG.

A BASKET WOVEN OF PALM LEAVES.

RIGHT: TUAMOTU PEARL DIVERS IN THE 1930S.

twenty feet of water with about eight oysters on each string. In a good year a small island like Raroia makes $350,000 from pearls with a cost of $50,000.

Raroia normally has a population of about 400 people, but presently only about sixty people are there and many of the houses are completely abandonned. Where did they all go? To Papeete, of course, not only to put the children in school, but to spend all their pearl money.

Raroia received recognition in 1947 when the *Kon-Tiki*, a Norwegian archeological expedition, first landed on its reef. A few years later, one of the expedition's anthropologists, Bengt Danielsson, returned to stay for a year to write *Raroia, Happy Island of the South Seas*, which described life on a Tuamotu island.

"There are no street noises, no noise of machinery, the nearest telephone is 470 miles away, newspapers are unknown, and no one uses a clock except as an ornament…. Another refreshing experience in life on Raroia is its independence. We have no hours to keep, no duties that call us, no etiquette, no fashions to follow, and no other relations with our fellow men than those which friendship dictates."

Water is scarce, making life hard in the Tuamotus. Fresh fruits and vegetables are almost nonexistent, and a diet of fish, coconuts, rice, and canned food is quickly tiring. Hurricanes are always to be feared. Waves from these fierce winds can cover the low islands, so that only by climbing the palm trees can the inhabitants keep from being swept out to sea.

The Islands of Disappointment

In 1765, when Commodore John Byron (the poet's grandfather) found Napuka and Tepoto, he named them the "Islands of Disappointment" because he could not find a particular grass which had a high content of Vitamin C, necessary to cure his men of scurvy.

Actually, these islands are not disappointing at all but beautiful atolls with friendly people. Until 1906, the people lived a traditional way of life. But after a large hurricane, the French government generously sent supplies to help out; it was the end of the old way of life. Now only a few islanders still know the traditional way of making fishhooks out of shell and bone.

Today, on Tepoto, some of the houses have solar energy and television. These luxuries reflect the profitability of copra, a plentiful crop that enables a man to make about $2,000 a month (government subsidized wages), much of which is spent on canned food. Despite an abundance of fish, the islanders eat canned corned beef and fish brought by the copra boat, until their supply runs out and they must go back to fishing. Their teeth are in deplorable condition because of a lack of vitamins and minerals in their diet.

Although the Tuamotu life has its hardships, it also has a certain tranquility to be found only on an atoll. Time stops. Nothing exists but the sea and the tiny strips of land with sand beaches. The chain of islands is small in land area, but like a string of pearls, its beauty cannot be measured in size.

There are two moments in a diver's life;
   One, when, a beggar, he prepares to plunge;
   Then, when, a prince, he rises with his pearl.

~ Frederick O'Brien, *Atolls of the Sun*

A PRIVATELY OWNED STRING OF PET OYSTERS CAN PRODUCE BLACK PEARLS SUCH AS THOSE ON THE RIGHT.

Left, top to bottom:
Church door,
Takaroa; Church
door, Raroia;
Church window,
Raroia.

God's best—at least God's sweetest works—Polynesians.

~ Robert Louis Stevenson

ABOVE: ON TEPOTO, ONE OF THE MOST REMOTE ISLANDS IN THE TUAMOTU ARCHIPELAGO. *RIGHT:* TYPICAL ATOLL CHURCH ON NAPUKA.

...they pass a large portion of their time in the arms of Somnus. ...to many of them, indeed, life is little else than an often interrupted and luxurious nap.

~ Herman Melville, *Typee*

The shark, finding that it was receiving no hurt, had become bolder. Several times it nearly got me, but each time Otoo was there just the moment before it was too late. Of course, Otoo could have saved himself any time. But he stuck by me. ...I changed my course and struck out blindly. I was by that time barely conscious. As my hand closed on the line I heard an exclamation from on board. I turned and looked. There was no sign of Otoo. The next instant he broke surface. Both hands were off at the wrist, the stumps spouting blood.

~ JACK LONDON, *SOUTH SEA TALES*

BOYS HOLDING THE TEETH OF THE FEARED *MAKO* SHARK.

FAR LEFT: BOY RIDING TWELVE-FOOT TIGER SHARK CAUGHT WITH HOOK AND LINE AND ABOUT TO EXPIRE. *LEFT:* GREY REEF SHARK.

But to see atoll life at its best you must go farther east beyond Tahiti, where there are so many low-lying islands that they seem to form clouds along the horizon. There the Polynesians have built a true island culture.

~ JAMES MICHENER, *RETURN TO PARADISE*

FISHING CANOES AND A SOCIETY EXPEDITIONS' SHIP ON TEPOTO.

In an age of anxiety men seek a refuge. Because of some deep urge, constant throughout history, troubled men tradition- ally dream of islands, possibly because the smallness of an island invites the illusion that here the complexities of conti- nental societies can be avoided, or at least controlled. This is a permanent, world-wide dream.

~ JAMES MICHENER AND A. GROVE DAY,

RASCALS IN PARADISE

RIGHT: SCARCITY OF FOOD MAKES CANINES INTO GOOD "FISHERDOGS." DOGS ARE EATEN AS A DELICACY THROUGHOUT POLYNESIA. EVEN CAPTAIN COOK TRIED IT AND COMMENTED, "IT DID NOT MUCH DIFFER FROM ENGLISH LAMB." *BELOW RIGHT:* "THE DANGEROUS ISLANDS", SO CALLED BECAUSE MANY SHIPS HAVE WRECKED ON THE REEFS WHICH SURROUND THE ISLANDS.

…the colors of which can only
be compared to those of precious stones or of humming-
birds—geranium reds, chinese
greens, blues one would not
know how to paint—and a host
of little creatures striped with all
the shades of the rainbow,
having the form of everything
except that of fish.

~ PIERRE LOTI, *THE MARRIAGE OF LOTI*

COPRA (DRIED COCONUT MEAT) HAS BEEN THE LARGEST EXPORT OF POLYNESIA FOR A CENTURY. THE COCONUT OIL FROM COPRA IS USED IN SUNTAN LOTION, SOAP, SHAMPOO, AND PERFUME.

HUSKING AND SCRAPING OUT THE WHITE INSIDES OF COCONUTS IS HARD LABOR.

The wise traveller travels only in imagination. An old Frenchman (he was really a Savoyard) once wrote a book called *Voyage Autour de ma Chambre....* Those are the best journeys, the journeys that you take at your own fireside, for then you lose none of your illusions.

~ W. SOMERSET MAUGHAM, *THE TREMBLING OF A LEAF*

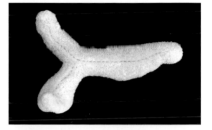

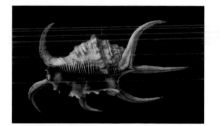

LEFT: AT THE END OF THE
EIGHTEENTH CENTURY,
XAVIER DE MAISTRE WROTE
*VOYAGE AUTOUR DE MA
CHAMBRE.* INSPIRED BY
PAINTINGS, BOOKS AND
LETTERS, HE SPENT FORTY-
TWO DAYS IN HIS ROOM
IMAGINING FANTASTIC
JOURNEYS FROM THE POLES
TO CORAL ATOLLS. HE DID
NOT SUFFER THE HARDSHIPS
HE WOULD HAVE IF HE
WENT TO THE TUAMOTUS.

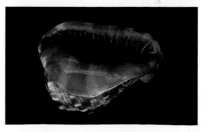

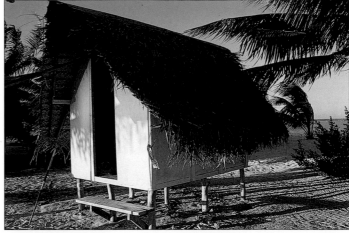

ABOVE TOP: PALM-THATCHED HOUSE WITH IMPORTED CORROGATED IRON ROOF.

ABOVE BOTTOM: HOUSE BUILT ENTIRELY OF THATCHED PALM FRONDS.

ABOVE TOP: PLYWOOD HOUSE, PALM-THATCHED ROOF.

ABOVE BOTTOM: ANCIENT POLYNESIAN STONE TEMPLE ON RAROIA CONVERTED INTO A CATHOLIC ALTAR.

LEFT: TUAMOTU BOY BATHES IN THE WARMTH OF ETERNAL SUMMER. *OPPOSITE PAGE:* COPRA SCHOONER CAPTAIN NAVIGATES THROUGH A DANGEROUS, NARROW PASS IN THE REEF, TO THE SAFETY OF THE LAGOON.

E hari te fau,
E toro te faaro,
E no te taata.

The palm tree will flourish,
The coral will spread,
But man will perish.

~ ANCIENT POLYNESIAN PROVERB

THE MARQUESAS
GAUGUIN COUNTRY

*CHANCED TO PUSH ASIDE A BRANCH, AND BY SO
doing suddenly disclosed to my view a scene
which even now I can recall with all the
vividness of the first impression. Had a glimpse
of the gardens of Paradise been revealed to me,
I could scarcely have been more ravished with
the sight.*

Then, Herman Melville descended into the
dreaded valley of the Typees and met the
cannibals: *I paused for a second, and I know
not by what impulse it was that I answered,
"Typee." The piece of dusky statuary nodded
in approval, and then murmured,
"Mortarkee?" "Mortarkee," said I, without
further hesitation—"Typee mortarkee."... When this commotion had
a little subsided, the principal chief squatted once more before me, and
throwing himself into a sudden rage, poured forth a string of philippics,
which I was at no loss to understand, from the frequent recurrence of
the word Happar, as being directed against the natives of the adjoining
valley. In all these denunciations my companion and I acquiesced,
while we extolled the character of the warlike Typees....*

*From the rest of these, however, I must except the beauteous nymph
Fayaway, who was my peculiar favourite. Her free pliant figure was the
very perfection of female grace and beauty. Her complexion was a rich
and mantling olive, and when watching the glow upon her cheeks I
could almost swear that beneath the transparent medium there lurked
the blushes of a faint vermilion. The face of this girl was a rounded oval,
and each feature as perfectly formed as the heart or imagination of man
could desire. Her full lips, when parted with a smile, disclosed teeth of
a dazzling whiteness; and when her rosy mouth opened with a burst of
merriment, they looked like the milk-white seeds of the "arta," a fruit
of the valley, which, when cleft in twain, shows them reposing in rows*

on either side, embedded in the red and juicy pulp.... Though in my eyes, at least, Fayaway was indisputably the loveliest female I saw in Typee, yet the description I have given of her will in some measure apply to nearly all the youthful portion of her sex in the valley. Judge ye then, reader, what beautiful creatures they must have been.

~HERMAN MELVILLE, *TYPEE*

The Marquesas Islands lie 850 miles northeast of Tahiti and consist of Nuku Hiva, Hiva Oa, Ua Pou, Fatu Hiva, Ua Huka, Tahuata, Motane, and Eiao. Judging from old pottery, the Marquesas were settled as early as 150 B.C. Archeologists have found that certain Marquesan pottery was made with clay that only comes from a particular valley in Fiji. That island was on the long route that the first Indo-Asians took to reach the Marquesas.

The first European to discover the Marquesas was Alvardo de Mendaña, who named the islands after the Marques de Mendosa, Viceroy of Peru in 1595. The Spaniards killed several hundred natives.

In 1813, David Porter arrived to begin a fifteen-month stay, claiming the island of Nuku Hiva for the United States and building Fort Madison. Porter's settlement in the Marquesas was not successful, and he killed off more natives.

In 1842, Herman Melville deserted the ship *Acushnet* (called the *Dolly* in his novel *Typee*) and lived amongst the remote Taipis, writing the most accurate and last account of the true, ancient Polynesian life.

Melville arrived at Taiohae Bay at the same time that the Marquesas were claimed for France by Admiral Dupetit-Thouars: *There seemed to be no cares, griefs, troubles, or vexations in all Typee... no foreclosures of mortgages, no protested notes, no bills payable, no debts to honour,... no duns of any description; no assault and battery attorneys,... no destitute widows with their children starving on the cold charities of the world; no beggars; no debtor's prisons; no proud and hard-hearted nabobs in Typee; or, to sum up all in one word—no*

Money!... All was mirth, fun, and high good humour.

Over forty-six years later, Robert Louis Stevenson sailed in on his yacht *Casco* and found the Marquesans quite decimated. In the early years, there were about 20,000 people in the Marquesas; disease and violence had reduced them to 5,000 people.

In 1891, Paul Gauguin went to Tahiti to paint, leaving behind in Europe his wife, two children, and a job as a stockbroker in Paris. After several years of painting and writing *Noa Noa*, he attempted suicide, burdened by financial and health problems. Finding Tahiti too civilized, he moved to the remote Marquesas, to the primitive mystical life he sought, hung a sign over the door of his new two-story studio: *La Maison du Jouir* (The House of Pleasure), and was inspired to work again. Finally, he received some recognition and money from Paris. In 1903, only two years after his arrival, he died on the island of Hiva Oa. The Marquesans loved and respected Gauguin, who fought for their human rights against the *bourgeois* officials of the town, Atuona. When Gauguin died, the chief cried, "Koke (Gauguin's nickname) is dead, now we are all lost." Gauguin requested one of his favorite works, a statue of *Oviri moe-ahere* (the savage who sleeps in the forest), a god of death, be placed at his grave. The statue has a revealing figure suggesting fertility, other-worldly large eyes, and she clutches a wolf cub; at her feet lies a dead bloody wolf, an allegory of life and death.

Shortly after the turn of the century, Jack London designed and built his yacht the *Snark* in San Francisco. In 1907, he sailed it to Nuku Hiva, finding the people on the point of extinction. By the 1920s, only 1,200 people remained on these islands. At one point, the magnificent Taipi people dwindled down to a population of only twelve.

Today, about 150 people live in Taipi Valley, working copra. The numerous abandoned *paepae* (stone structures), statues, and other artifacts are sad reminders of what was once an intricate and artistic civilization.

On the far side of the island, in the district of Puamau, are the giant stone *tiki* which are comparable to the magnificent statues on Easter Island. Scientists can only estimate the origin of these statues. The largest, Takaii, is eight feet tall and is covered with detailed petroglyphs, which are hard to see because of all the lichen and moss.

The Marquesas early acquired a reputation as the home of cannibals. Melville's work reflects this facet of island life, as does the work of Robert Louis Stevenson.

Nothing more strongly arouses our disgust than cannibalism, nothing so surely unmortars a society; nothing, we might plausibly argue, will so harden and degrade the minds of those that practise it. And yet we ourselves make much the same appearance in the eyes of the Buddhist and the vegetarian.... The Marquesans intertwined man-eating with the whole texture of their lives; long-pig was in a sense their currency and sacrament; it formed the hire of the artist, illustrated public events, and was the occasion and attraction of a feast....

Of one such exploit I can give the account of an eye-witness. 'Portuguese Joe,' Mr. Keane's cook, was once pulling an oar in an Atuona boat, when they spied a stranger in a canoe with some fish and a piece of tapa. The Atuona men cried upon him to draw near and have a smoke. He complied, because, I suppose, he had no choice; but he knew, poor devil, what he was coming to, and (as Joe said) 'he didn't seem to care about the smoke.'... And then, of a sudden, a big fellow in Joe's boat leaned over, plucked the stranger from his canoe, struck him with a knife in the neck—inward and downward, as Joe showed in pantomime more expressive than his words—and held him under water, like a fowl, until his struggles ceased. Whereupon the long-pig was hauled on board, the boat's head turned about for Atuona, and these Marquesan braves pulled home rejoicing.

~ ROBERT LOUIS STEVENSON, *IN THE SOUTH SEAS*

MARQUESANS DRAWN AFTER W. TILESIUS FROM KRUSENSTERN'S VOYAGE IN 1803. THE MAN SECOND FROM THE TOP IS JEAN-BAPTISTE CABRI, A EUROPEAN BEACHCOMBER WHO TURNED NATIVE. EVENTUALLY, HE RETURNED TO EUROPE WHERE HE DANCED AND SHOWED HIS "SAVAGE" TATTOOS FOR A LIVING.

There is only one regular mode of transportation to the island of Fatu Hiva: a copra boat once a month. There is no airport and there are only a couple of cars on this southernmost island of the Marquesan chain.

When a yacht arrives in Fatu Hiva's Hanavavae Bay—The Bay of Virgins, a majestic anchorage ringed by jagged cliffs—canoes full of natives paddle out with sacks of oranges, lemons, breadfruit, stocks of bananas, slabs of wild goat and boar meat, and *tapa* cloth with intricate designs—just as in Robert Louis Stevenson's day—however, the natives now trade for music cassettes, T-shirts, and sunglasses.

On the hill overlooking Vaitahu Village, on Tahuata, are the remnants of small forts built by the French in 1842. On the walls are scraps of graffiti, soldiers' names, and the typical observations: *Amiral Dupetit-Thouars est un emmerdeur.*

On the waterfront is a small monument commemorating the few French soldiers who died when the Marquesas were proclaimed a French territory. It's odd that the plaque commemorates only the French soldiers, but an old islander once observed, "None of the Marquesans died in the battle. We were smart warriors; we hid behind the rocks."

Fortunately, the French are credited in preserving the Marquesas, and not commercially exploiting them. There are no malls, stop lights, large hotels, or theme parks—just valleys and beaches in overwhelming nature.

Although the Marquesas are mysterious and lugubrious, their beauty is majestic and the most awe inspiring of the fabled isles of the South Seas.

A HUMAN SACRIFICE AT OTAHEITE WITNESSED BY CAPTAIN JAMES COOK IN 1777. DRAWN BY JOHN WEBBER, ARTIST ON THE SECOND VOYAGE OF THE *RESOLUTION*. SACRIFICES TOOK PLACE ON MANY ISLANDS IN POLYNESIA, PARTICULARLY IN THE MARQUESAS. COOK WAS KILLED AND PARTIALLY DEVOURED IN 1779 BY HAWAIIANS, WHO DISCOVERED HE WAS NOT THE DEMIGOD *LONO* THEY HAD THOUGHT HIM TO BE. THE DEATH OF CAPTAIN COOK INCREASED EUROPEANS' FASCINATION WITH THE SOUTH SEAS; HOWEVER, THE VIEW OF THE NOBLE SAVAGE WAS CHANGED. THE WIDELY PUBLICIZED REPORTS OF EXPLORERS GAVE LITTLE SUPPORT TO DIDEROT'S AND ROUSSEAU'S IDYLLIC THEORIES ON THE VIRTUES OF ARCADIA. WITH INFANTICIDE, CANNIBALISM, AND THIEVERY, THIS NATURAL WORLD WAS PERHAPS NO BETTER THAN THE CIVILIZED ONE.

"Fire!" exclaimed I, while my heart took to beating like a triphammer, "what fire?"

"Why, the fire to cook us, to be sure; what else would the cannibals be kicking up such a row about, if it were not for that?" … Suddenly the silence was broken by the well-remembered tones of Mehevi, and at the kindly accents of his voice, my fears were immediately dissipated. "Tommo, Toby, ki ki!" (eat). He had waited to address us, until he had assured himself that we were both awake, at which he seemed somewhat surprised.

"Ki ki! is it?" said Toby, in his gruff tones; "well, cook us first, will you—but what's this?"… "A baked baby, by the soul of Captain Cook!" burst forth Toby, with amazing

CENTER: A BOY CARRYING A YOUNG BOAR. TRAINED DOGS TRACK AND ATTACK THE BOAR; FINALLY, THE HUNTER KILLS IT WITH A MACHETE. *BELOW:* AFTER THE HUNT.

BELOW: SLICING OPEN AN ORANGE DURING A REST WHILE HUNTING WILD BOAR.

vehemence. "Veal? why, there never was a calf on the island till you landed…. When the taper came, I gazed eagerly into the vessel, and recognized the mutilated remains of a juvenile porker! "Puarkee!" exclaimed Kory-Kory, looking complacently at the dish; and from that day to this I have never forgotten that such is the designation of a pig in the Typee lingo.

~ HERMAN MELVILLE, *Typee*

CHILDREN OF THE MARQUESAS STILL PLAY A GAME OF STILTS AS THEY HAVE DONE SINCE THE GAME WAS WITNESSED BY THE EARLIEST EXPLORERS.

The boys play horses exactly as we do in Europe; and have very good fun on stilts, trying to knock each other down, in which they do not often succeed.

~ ROBERT LOUIS STEVENSON, *LETTER TO THOMAS ARCHER, NOVEMBER 1888*

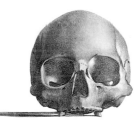

FAR RIGHT: TAHIA MOMO OPENING HER MAIL IN FRONT OF THE POST OFFICE IN OMOA, FATU HIVA. SHE IS THE DAUGHTER OF TEI, THE LAST KNOWN CANNIBAL, AND WAS THE LITTLE GIRL IN THOR HEYERDHAL'S BOOK *FATU-HIVA*, 1936. TEI DESCRIBED HUMAN FLESH AS TASTING LIKE RIPE BANANAS.

LEFT: LOADING SUPPLIES IS ACCOMPLISHED TODAY AS IT WAS IN THE PAST. AN OUTBOARD ENGINE HELPS A LITTLE. SMALL BOATS RIDE IN THROUGH THE SURF TO DELIVER IMPORTS ON REMOTE ISLANDS THROUGHOUT THE SOUTH SEAS. *BELOW LEFT:* UNLOADING SUPPLIES ON THE BEACH IN UA POU. *BELOW:* ANCIENT FISH HOOK. MOST WERE MADE FROM SHELLS OR HUMAN BONES.

Soon they began to come, swinging along the trail below us at a gait between a walk and a trot. The younger men carried four or five bunches each; the older ones from six to eight, the weight being nicely adjusted on their poles. Faiipo came last. He sauntered along lazily, humming a little tune, and with such a load that I forgot for the moment the mosquitoes. He carried a burden of well over three hundred pounds!

~ ROBERT DEAN FRISBIE, *MY TAHITI*, 1924

POLYNESIAN MAN CARRYING A LOAD OF *FEI* (MOUNTAIN BANANAS), CIRCA EARLY 1900s.

BOY CARRYING A
LOAD OF MOUNTAIN
BANANAS ON FATU
HIVA.

But here it does no harm, for children are welcome and are spoken for in advance by all the relatives. It's a struggle as to who should be the mother and father nurses. A child is the most beautiful present one can give.

~ PAUL GAUGUIN,
THE LETTERS OF PAUL GAUGUIN

CHILDREN WAITING
TO SEE THE DENTIST
IN THE REMOTE
HAKATEHAU VALLEY
ON UA POU.

THE COUNTRY DENTIST PULLING DECAYED TEETH IN A REMOTE VALLEY ON UA POU, ACCESSIBLE ONLY BY BOAT. ONCE KNOWN FOR THEIR WHITE TEETH, POLYNESIANS ARE NOW NOTORIOUS FOR THE LACK OF GOOD TEETH, CAUSED BY THEIR DIET AND POOR DENTAL HYGIENE.

Left: SPOONS CARVED BY PAUL GAUGUIN. INSPIRED BY MARQUESAN WOOD CARVERS, GAUGUIN SET UP A SCULPTURE STUDIO ON THE GROUND FLOOR OF HIS HOUSE, MASTERING THE ART OF SCULPTING BOWLS, UTENSILS, AND FIGURES WITH INTRICATE DETAILS. *Above:* MODERN MARQUESAN BOWL MADE FROM A COCONUT.

PAUL GAUGUIN, INSPIRED BY THE ROUSSEAUEAN MYTH AND PIERRE LOTI, CAME TO TAHITI AND SUBSEQUENTLY SETTLED IN THE MARQUESAS TO PAINT WHAT REMAINED OF THE LIFE OF THE NOBLE SAVAGE.

A SMALL STATUE IS AT GAUGUIN'S GRAVE, ON THE HILL ABOVE ATUONA. ON THE PEDESTAL IS WRITTEN "*OVIRI*" (SAVAGE), A GOD OF DEATH AND MOURNING. NEARBY LIES THE GRAVE OF THE ACTOR AND SONGWRITER JACQUES BREL.

DRAWING BY ESKRIDGE, OF EMILE GAUGUIN, THE SON OF PAUL, AS A YOUNG MAN IN 1931. LATER, HE MADE CHILDLIKE PAINTINGS AND FISHTRAPS SIGNED *BY GAUGUIN* FOR TOURISTS.

Opposite page right: RARE PHOTO OF VAITE GOUPIL. *Center:* GAUGUIN'S PAINTING OF VAITE. *Far right:* RECEIPT FROM GAUGUIN TO MR. GOUPIL AN ENTREPRENEUR FOR 36 FRANCS FOR THE PAINTING. TODAY, GAUGUIN PAINTINGS SELL FOR TEN MILLION DOLLARS.

From floor to ceiling the walls were covered with a strange and elaborate composition. It was indescribably wonderful and mysterious. It took his breath away. It filled him with an emotion which he could not understand or analyse. He felt the awe and the delight which a man might feel who watched the beginning of a world. It was tremendous, sensual, passionate; and yet there was something horrible there, too, something which made him afraid. It was the work of a man who had delved into the hidden depths of nature and had discovered secrets which were beautiful and fearful too. It was the work of a man who knew things which it is unholy for men to know. There was something primeval there and terrible. It was not human. It brought to his mind vague recollections of black magic. It was beautiful and obscene.

"*Mon Dieu*, this is genius."

~ W. SOMERSET MAUGHAM,
THE MOON AND SIXPENCE

ABOVE: TE RERIOA (THE DAY DREAM) REFLECTS THE MYSTERY OF POLYNESIANS THAT FASCINATED GAUGUIN. THE NATIVES IN GAUGUIN'S PAINTINGS NEVER SMILE BUT SEEM TO BE THINKING OF THEIR MYSTERIOUS AND LOST PAST. THE WALLS OF THE HOUSE ARE PAINTED IN THE SAME MANNER AS GAUGUIN'S OWN HOUSE. *RIGHT:* WOOD BLOCK PRINTS BY PAUL GAUGUIN.

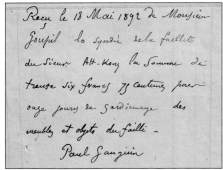

They had the grace and elasticity of healthy young animals. A mingled perfume, half animal, half vegetable emanated from them; the perfume of their blood and of the gardenias—*tiaré*—which all wore in their hair. "*Téiné merahi noa noa* (now very fragrant)," they said.

~ PAUL GAUGUIN, *NOA NOA*

The life is so serene, so
favourable to art-work,
that it is madness to seek
for anything else... .
~ PAUL GAUGUIN,
*THE LETTERS OF PAUL GAUGUIN TO
GEORGES DANIEL DE MONFREID*

OPPOSITE PAGE: PHOTO
OF GIRL HOLDING A
FRUIT BASKET, 1989. *THIS
PAGE: DEUX
TAHITIENNES* PAINTED BY
PAUL GAUGUIN IN 1889.
COURTESY OF
METROPOLITAN
MUSEUM OF ART, NEW
YORK.

LEFT: BOY IN A TREE PICKING RIPE BREADFRUIT. WHEN COLLECTING BREADFRUIT, ONE PERSON THROWS THE BREADFRUIT DOWN WHILE ANOTHER SKILLFULLY CATCHES IT WITH A BURLAP SACK.

ABOVE: MARQUESAN WOMAN OF HIVA OA COOKING LUNCH, THE MAIN MEAL OF THE DAY. WITH A STICK, SHE TURNS BREADFRUIT WHICH IS SIMPLY PLACED OVER OR IN THE FIRE. IT ALSO TASTES GOOD, SLICED AND DEEP FRIED.

ARTOCARPUS ALTILIS, BREADFRUIT, *URU*

TOP TO BOTTOM: A SPROUTING BREADFRUIT. UNRIPE BREADFRUIT. RIPE *URU* (BREADFRUIT). IT IS INEDIBLE UNLESS COOKED. SLICING COOKED BREADFRUIT. IT TASTES SIMILAR TO BREAD AND SWEET POTATOES.
OPPOSITE PAGE: MARQUESAN MAN TATTOOED IN THE MARQUESAN STYLE, FROM HEAD TO FOOT!

In the article of food these happy people may almost be said to be exempt from the curse of our forefathers; scarcely can it be said that they earn their bread by the sweat of their brow, when their chief sustenance, breadfruit, is procured with no more trouble than that of climbing a tree, and pulling it down.

~ SIR JOSEPH BANKS,
JOURNAL OF THE RT HON SIR JOSEPH BANKS (1769), 1768-71

Above: The ancient art of tattooing, which is practiced throughout Polynesia. The artist is tattooing the man's buttock. *Below:* A Marquesan woman being tattooed while a man enters with a boar's head as payment. Engraving after Von Krusenstern's voyage in 1803.

On entering the thicket, I witnessed for the first time the operation of tattooing as performed by these islanders.

I beheld a man extended flat upon his back, on the ground, and, despite the forced composure of his countenance, it was evident that he was suffering agony. His tormentor bent over him, working away for all the world like a stone-cutter with

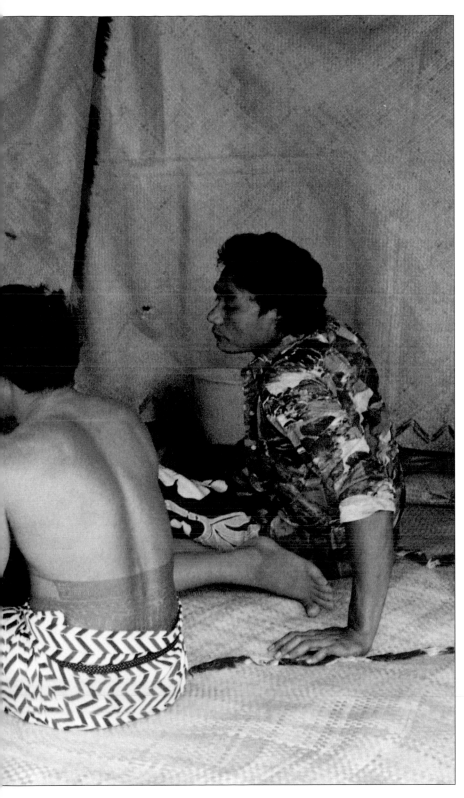

MANY POLYNESIANS
WERE TATTOOED AT
PUBERTY. IT WAS A
MARK OF MATURITY,
REFINEMENT, AND
ARTISTIC BEAUTY.
CHARLES DARWIN
NOTED, "THAT THEY
HAVE A VERY ELEGANT
EFFECT." MANY OF
CAPTAIN COOK'S MEN
WERE TATTOOED,
INCLUDING THE
FAMOUS BOTANIST SIR
JOSEPH BANKS; THE
WEALTHY DAPPER
GENTLEMAN BECAME
THE RAGE OF LONDON
WHEN HE SHOWED HIS
TATTOOED ARM AT TEA
PARTIES. ON HIS
RETURN TO THE
SOUTH SEAS ABOARD
THE *BOUNTY*, HE WAS
OUTDONE BY
FLETCHER CHRISTIAN,
WHO HAD HIS ENTIRE
BUTTOCKS TATTOOED.

mallet and chisel. In one hand
he held a short slender stick,
pointed with a shark's tooth, on
the upright end of which he
tapped with a small hammer-
like piece of wood, thus punc-
turing the skin, and charging it
with the colouring matter in
which the instrument was
dipped.

~ HERMAN MELVILLE, *TYPEE*

At the turn of the land, Atuona came in view: a long beach, a heavy and loud breach of surf, a shore-side village scattered among trees, and the guttered mountains drawing near on both sides…I thought it the loveliest, and by far the most ominous and gloomy, spot on earth. Beautiful it surely was; and even more salubrious.

~ Robert Louis Stevenson, *In the South Seas*

TIARE
TAHITI

Hard for us to understand.
Out of time, beyond the sun,
All are one in Paradise,

There the Eternals are, and there
The Good, the Lovely, and the True,
And Types, whose earthly copies were
The foolish broken things we knew;
There is the Face, whose ghosts we are;
The real, the never-setting Star;
And the Flower, of which we love
Faint and fading shadows here;
Never a tear, but only Grief;

Dance, but not the limbs that move;
Songs in Song shall disappear;
Instead of lovers, Love shall be;
For hearts, Immutability;
And there, on the Ideal Reef,
Thunders the Everlasting Sea!

About the idle warm lagoon.
Hasten, hand in human hand,
Down the dark, the flowered way,
Along the whiteness of the sand,
And in the water's soft caress,
Wash the mind of foolishness,

Mamua, until the day.
Spend the glittering moonlight there
Pursuing down the soundless deep
Limbs that gleam and shadowy hair,
Or floating lazy, half-asleep.
Dive and double and follow after,
Snare in flowers, and kiss, and call,
With lips that fade, and human laughter
And faces individual,
Well this side of Paradise! …
There's little comfort in the wise.

~ RUPERT BROOKE,
THE COLLECTED POEMS OF RUPERT BROOKE

A'ahi: Tuna.

Ahu: Stone temples on Easter Island.

Aita peapea: No problem.

Aku Aku: Spirits or power in Easter Island.

Anakena: District of Easter Island.

Ananahi: Tomorrow.

Ana Kai Tangata: Cannibal cave on Easter Island.

Api: New.

Arearea: Amusement.

Ari'i: King, royal family.

Ata: Laugh.

Atua: God.

Aué: An exclamation of sorrow or pain, "Alas!"

E aha te huru?: How are you? Literally, what is the state of being?

E hia moni?: How much does it cost?

Faaa: District in Tahiti where the airport is located.

Fa'a'amu: To adopt a child.

Fa'a'apu: Plantation, to cultivate.

Fa'aipoipo: To marry.

Fare nihau: Pandanus local style house.

Fare purera'a: Church.

Fee fee: Elephantiasis.

Fei: Red mountain bananas, edible only when cooked.

Fenua: Land.

Feti'i: Relatives, family.

Fifiri: Figure eight donuts, made of flour and fried in oil.

Fiu: Fed up, bored.

Ha'ama: Embarrassed, ashamed.

Ha'ari: Coconut.

Haere: To move, go.

Haere mai namuri ia'u: Come, follow me.

Hambos: Young bums, usually found along the waterfront.

Hapu pape: To shower.

Heiva: Dance show.

Himene: To sing or a song.

Hinano: A type of flower.

Hina'aro: To want, like.

Hoe a te va'a: To paddle a canoe.

Iaorana: The common Tahitian greeting. Literally, "life to."

I'a ota: Marinated raw fish.

Kaamaina: Foreigner who has been on the island a long time.

Kai kai: To eat, in Marquesan; however, it is a common saying throughout the islands.

Kanahau: Good, in Marquesan.

Kaoha: Hello, in Marquesan.

Kavehu: Coconut crab.

Kiaora: Hello, in Paumotu.

Kiaorana: Hello, in the Cook Islands.

Maeva!: Welcome!

Mahi mahi: Dolphin.

Mahu: Transvestite.

Mai tai: Good.

Maitake: Good in the Cook Islands.

Mamu!: Be quiet!

Mana: Spiritual power.

Manu-tara: Sooty tern.

Marae: Temple, ceremonial place.

Mauruuru: Thank you.

Menahune: Ancient term for common people.

Mitiha'ari: Coconut cream used in Tahitian dishes.

Mitihue: Fermented coconut cream.

Moai: Stone statues on Easter Island.

Moana: Sea, ocean.

Moemoea: Dream.

Monoi: Coconut oil.

Motu: Island.

Nave nave: Sexy.

Nehenehe: Beautiful.

Noa noa: Fragrant.

Nohu: Poisonous stone fish.

Pae pae: Stone temples in the Marquesas.

Pareu: Cloth wraparound used by men and women.

Paumotu: The conquered or finished islands; the language and people of the Tuamotu Islands. *Tuamotu* means far away islands.

Pia to'eto'e: Cold beer.

Poe: A stiff pudding made from starch and fruit.

Popa'a: A foreigner, not including Chinese who are called *Tinito*.

Porinetia: Polynesia.

Rano raraku: Part of Easter Island where the quarry for the statues is.

Rapa Nui: Easter Island.

Rongo rongo: Ancient writings or hieroglyphics carved on boards.

Tahai: The large stone temple near the town of Hangaroa on Easter Island.

Taipi: A valley on the island of Nuku Hiva.

Takaii: The name of the eight-feet-tall statue on the island of Hiva Oa. It is the largest statue in French Polynesia.

Tama'a: To eat food or come eat.

Tama'ara'a: Dinner party, feast.

Tamure: Dance.

Tane: Man.

Tangata manu: Bird-man cult on Easter Island.

Tapu: Forbidden.

Taravana: Crazy.

Taure'are'a: Literally "Happy youths." The youth of Tahiti.

Tavana: Chief or mayor of island.

Tiare: Flower.

Tiare Tahiti: A sweet smelling white flower native of Tahiti.

Tifaifai: Quilts with designs of colorful cut-out material.

Tiurai: July and July festivals.

Toere: Hollow log used as a drum.

Tumu ha'ari: Coconut tree.

Tupa: Land crab.

Tupapau: Ghosts, spirits.

Uru: Breadfruit.

Va'a: Canoe.

Vahine: Woman.

Ve'ave'a: Hot.

Vi: Mango.

BIBLIOGRAPHY

Ball, Ian M. *Pitcairn: Children of Mutiny.* Boston: Little, Brown and Company, 1973.

Banks, Sir Joseph. *The Endeavour Journal of Joseph Banks 1768-1771.* Edited by J. C. Beaglehole. 2 volumes. Sydney: Angus and Robertson, 1962.

Barrow, Sir John. *A Description of Pitcairn's Island and its Inhabitants with an Authentic Account of the Mutiny of the Ship Bounty.* New York: J&J Harper, 1832.

The Mutiny & Piratical Seizure of H.M.S. Bounty. Oxford: Humpfrey Milford, Oxford University Press, 1831.

Becke, Louis. *South Sea Supercargo.* Edited with an introduction by A. Grove Day. Honolulu: University of Hawaii Press, 1967.

Bligh, William. *Bligh and the Bounty.* Unabridged edition of Bligh's narrative first published in 1792, with illustrations and a preface by Laurence Irving. New York: E.P. Dutton & Co., 1936.

Brooke, Rupert. *The Collected Poems of Rupert Brooke.* New York: Dodd, Mead & Company, 1915.

Cameron, Ian. *Lost Paradise.* Topsfield, Ma.: Salem House Publishers, 1987.

Carter, John. *Pacific Islands Year Book.* Sydney, New York: Pacific Publications, 1984.

Christian, Glynn. *Fragile Paradise.* Boston: Little, Brown and Company, 1982.

Coleridge, Samuel Taylor. *The Rime of the Ancient Mariner.* The Annotated Ancient Mariner. New York: Clarkson N. Potter Inc., 1965.

Conrad, Barnaby. *Tahiti.* New York: The Viking Press, 1962.

Cook, Captain James. 9 volumes of his voyages. Original editions. London: W. Strahan and T. Cadell, 1773-1780.

Danielsson, Bengt. *Gauguin in the South Seas.* Translated from the Swedish. New York: Doubleday & Company, 1966.

———.*Love in the South Seas.* New York: Reynal & Company, 1956.

———. *Moruroa, Mon Amour.* England: Penguin Books, 1977.

———.*Raroia. Happy Island of the South Seas.* New York: Rand McNally & Company, 1953.

———.*Tahiti. Circle Island Tour Guide.* Papeete, Tahiti: Les Editions du Pacifique, 1976.

Darwin, Charles. *The Voyage of the Beagle.* London: J.M. Dent & Sons, 1906.

Dening, Greg. *Islands and Beaches.* Honolulu: The University Press of Hawaii, 1980.

Dodd, Edward. *Polynesian Seafaring.* New York: Dodd, Mead & Company, 1972.

———.*The Rape of Tahiti.* New York: Dodd, Mead & Company, 1983.

Dos Passos, John. *Easter Island. Island of Enigmas.* New York: Doubleday & Company, 1971.

Eggleston, George T. *Tahiti, Voyage through Paradise*. New York: The Devin-Adair Company, 1953.

Eskridge, Robert Lee. *Mangareva*. Indianapolis: The Bobbs-Merrill Company, 1931.

Frisbee, Johnny. *The Frisbees of the South Seas*. New York: Doubleday & Company, 1959.

Frisbee, Robert Dean. *My Tahiti*. Boston: Little, Brown and Company, 1937.

Furnas, J.C. *Anatomy of Paradise*. New York: William Sloane Associates, 1947.

Gauguin, Paul. *Intimate Journals*. Translated by Van Wyck Brooks. Indiana University Press, 1958.

————.*Noa Noa*. Translated from the French by O. F. Theis. New York: Greenberg Publisher, 1929.

————.*The Letters of Paul Gauguin to Georges Daniel de Monfreid*. Translated by Ruth Pielkovo. New York: Dodd, Mead & Company, 1922.

Grey, Zane. *The Reef Girl*. New York: Harper & Row, 1977.

Hall, James Norman. *Lost Island*. Boston: Little, Brown and Company, 1944.

————.*My Island Home*. Boston: Little, Brown and Company, 1952.

Hall, James Norman and Nordhoff, Charles Bernard. *Faery Lands of the South Seas*. New York: Garden City Publishing Co., 1921.

Henri, Teuira. *Ancient Tahiti*. Honolulu: Bishop Museum, 1928.

Heyerdahl, Thor. *Aku-Aku*. New York: Rand McNally & Co., 1958.

————.*Easter Island. The Mystery Solved*. New York: Random House, 1989.

————.*Fatu-Hiva. Back to Nature*. New York: Doubleday & Company, 1974.

————.*Kon-Tiki*. New York: Rand McNally & Co., 1950.

Howard, Michael. *Gauguin*. New York: Dorling Kindersley, Inc., 1992.

Howarth, David. *Tahiti. A Paradise Lost*. New York: The Viking Press, 1984.

Joppien, Rüdiger and Smith, Bernard. *The Art of Captain Cook's Voyages*. New Haven and London: Yale University Press, 1988.

Kennedy, Gavin. *Bligh*. London: Gerald Duckworth & Co., 1978.

Krusenstern, A. J. von. *Voyage Around the World*. Volumes I-II. London, 1813.

de La Pérouse, Jean-François Galaup. *A Voyage Round the World Performed in the Years 1785, 1786, 1787, and 1788 by the Boussole and Astrolabe*. Translated from the French. London: Lackington, Allen and Co., 1807.

London, Jack. *South Sea Tales*. New York: McKinlay, Stone & Mackenzie, 1911.

————. *The Cruise of the Snark*. New York: The Macmillan Company, 1911.

Loti, Pierre. *The Marriage of Loti*. Translated from the French by Wright and Eleanor Frierson. Honolulu: The University Press of Hawaii, 1976.

Marshall, Donald. *Raivavae*. New York: Doubleday & Company, 1961.

Maude, H. E. *Slavers in Paradise*. Suva, Fiji: University of the South Pacific, 1986.

Maugham, W. Somerset. *The Moon and Sixpence*. Groset & Dunlap, 1919.

————.*The Trembling of a Leaf*. New York: George H. Doran Company, 1921.

Mead, Margaret. *Coming of Age in Samoa*. Morrow Quill Paperbacks, 1961.

Melville, Herman. *Moby Dick*. New York, 1851.

————.*Omoo: A Narrative of Adventures in the South Seas*. New York, 1847.

————.*Typee: A Peep at Polynesian Life*. England: Penguin Books, 1972.

Michener, James A. *Rascals in Paradise*. New York: Random House, 1957.

————.*Return to Paradise*. New York: Random House, 1951.

————.*Tales of the South Pacific*. New York: The Macmillan Company, 1947.

Moorehead, Alan. *The Fatal Impact: The Invasion of the South Pacific, 1767-1840*. New York: Harper & Row Publishers, 1966.

Mortimer, George. *Observations and Remarks Made During a Voyage*. London: 1791.

Murray, Rev. Thos. Boyles. *Pitcairn: The Island, the People, and the Pastor*. London: Society for Promoting Christian Knowledge, 1853.

Nordhoff, Charles. *No More Gas*. Boston: Little, Brown and Company, 1940.

Nordhoff, Charles and Hall, James Norman. *Men Against the Sea*. Boston: Little, Brown and Company, 1934.

————.*Mutiny on the Bounty*. Boston: Little, Brown and Company, 1932.

————.*The Dark River*. Boston: Little, Brown and Company, 1938.

————.*The Hurricane*. Boston: Little, Brown and Company, 1936.

O'Brien, Frederick. *Atolls of the Sun*. New York: The Century Co., 1922.

————.*Mystic Isles of the South Seas*. New York: Garden City Publishing Company, 1921.

————.*White Shadows in the South Seas*. New York: The Century Co., 1919.

Orliac, Catherine and Michel. *Easter Island, Mystery of the Stone Giants*. New York: Harry N. Abrams, Inc., 1995.

Salvat, Bernard and Rives, Claude. *Shells of Tahiti*. Papeete, Tahiti: Les Editions du Pacifique, 1984.

Shapiro, H. L. *Heritage of the Bounty*. New York: Simon & Shuster, 1936.

Snow, Philip and Waine, Stefanie. *The People from the Horizon*. Oxford: Phaidon Press, 1979.

Stevenson, Robert Louis. *In the South Seas.* Being an account of experiences and observations in the Marquesas, Paumotus and Gilbert Islands. Facsimile Reproduction. Honolulu: University of Hawaii Press, 1971.

————.*Island Nights Entertainments*. New York: Charles Scribners' Sons, 1893.

————.*The Complete Short Stories of Robert Louis Stevenson*. Edited and with an introduction by Charles Neider. New York: Doubleday & Company, 1969.

Stoddard, Charles Warren. *The Island of Tranquil Delights*. Boston: Herbert B. Turner & Company, 1904.

Suggs, Robert C. *Marquesan Sexual Behavior*. New York: Harcourt, Brace & World, Inc., 1966.

Syme, Ronald. *The Lagoon Is Lonely Now*. Wellington, New Zealand: Millwood Press, 1978.

Twain, Mark. *Prose Poem on Hawaii*. Honolulu: 1954.

————.*The Stolen White Elephant*. 1882.

Varady, Ralph. *Many Lagoons*. New York: William Morrow and Co., 1958.

Waugh, Alec. *My Place in the Bazaar*. New York: Bantam Books, Inc., 1963.

Williams, John. *A Narrative of Missionary Enterprises in the South Sea Islands*. London: 1837.

Wilson, James. *A Missionary Voyage to the Southern Pacific Ocean Performed 1796-98 in the Ship Duff*. London: 1799.

Yapp, Peter. *The Traveller's Dictionary of Quotation*. London, Boston, Melbourne and Henley: Rouledge & Kegan Paul.

Young, Gavin. *Slow Boats Home*. New York: Random House, 1986.

Young, Rosalind Amelia. *Mutiny of the Bounty and the Story of Pitcairn Island*. Oakland, California: Pacific Press Publishing Company, 1894.

A HOUSE SET
ON A COCONUT
PLANTATION
IN OPUNOHU BAY,
MOOREA.
THE OWNER IS AN
AMERICAN, AN OLD
KAAMAINA (RESIDENT
OF THE ISLANDS FOR A
LONG TIME).

Malden

Starbuck

Victoria

Fatuhuhu · Coral Is
Hiau · · Clark Bk
Motuiti · Uauka
Nukahiva · MARQU
Uapu
Hivao
Tauata · Motan
Fatuh

Tongareva
or Penrhyn

Caroline

Rakahanga
Manihiki
Vostock

Pukapuka or
Danger
Tema Rf.
Nassau I.
Flint I.

Souwaroff I.

Tetopoto · Napuka
Mahini · Takaroa
Ahii · Apataka · Puka
Mataiiva · Aratika · Talume · Angatau
Tikahau · Kauehi · Fakaina
Bellinghausen · Tupai · Rangiroa · Arutua · Apataka
Scilly · Maupiti · Porapora · Toau · Raraka · Raroia
Mopelia · Tahaa · Huahine · Fakarava · Makemo
Raiatea · Tetuaroa · Tahanea · Marutea
SOCIETY ISLANDS · Tahiti · Anaa · Tauere · Tatai
Tapuaimanu · Maitea · Motutunga · Hikuero · Amanu
Ravahere · Akiaki
Nengonengo · Hao · Nukuta
Vairaatea · Vahit
Palmerston · Hereheretua · Pinaki

Aitutake
Auotu · Anuanuraro · Kukutipipi · Turei
Manuae · Anuanurunga · Vanavana
Mitiaro · Tematangi · Tengrunga
veridge Rf · Atiu · Mauke
COOK ISLANDS · Mururoa · Ahunu
Rarotonga · Hull Is · Morane
Mangaia · Rurutu
Rimatara · AUSTRAL ISL·DS
Tubuai · Ravaivai or · S. Juan B
Vavitao

Neilson Rf.

Haymet Rks

Orne Bk
Rapa or Rapaiti
Bass Is

It Began with Jenny

A HISTORY OF AIR TRANSPORTATION

WRITTEN AND ILLUSTRATED BY

It
Began
with
Jenny

JOHN EVERDS

Hubbard Press / NORTHBROOK, ILLINOIS

CONTENTS

Copyright © 1972, Hubbard Press, Northbrook, Illinois 60062

Library of Congress Catalog Card Number 72-83030

International Standard Book Number 0-8331-0011-4

Printed in the United States of America

CHAPTER ONE

The Beginning of Airmail Service

When you hear the whine of a big jetliner and watch it streak across the night sky, do you sometimes wonder how air travel began?

We all know that flying—powered flight—started with the Wright brothers. But air travel and the airlines began with "Jenny."

Let's go back to the year 1918 at Potomac Park in Washington, D.C. It is a bright, sunny morning in May. Potomac Park has become an airfield. Out on this field sits Jenny. Her proper name is Curtiss JN-4, and she's a mustard yellow biplane, a maze of wires and struts. There's excitement in the air, because the United States Post Office is about to start regular airmail service between Washington, Philadelphia, and New York City. Jenny is being loaded with the first four sacks of mail.

Important spectators line the field to watch the preparations. President and Mrs. Woodrow Wilson are there, with Postmaster General Burleson, Franklin D. Roosevelt (who was then the Assistant Secretary of the Navy) and the Postmaster General of Japan.

Everything seems to be ready. The pilot squeezes into the cockpit. A mechanic swings the propeller to start the engine. The pilot yells, "Contact! Switch on!" The engine coughs, sputters, and dies. President Wilson frowns and looks at his watch, thinking of pressing engagements back at the White House.

8

The propeller is swung again and again, but nothing happens. Finally someone discovers the gas tank is empty! Frantically, the tank is refilled, and once again the mechanic swings the propeller. This time Jenny responds. The engine barks and comes alive! The pilot, already fifteen minutes behind schedule, pushes the throttle forward. Jenny bounces across the park grounds, barely clearing the trees at the edge of the field. The airmail is on its way north to Philadelphia and New York. Well, almost. It seems that the pilot has lost all sense of direction. Bewildered bystanders see Jenny heading south.

Several hours later the pilot phones to report that he has landed, tail up, 25 miles away on a Maryland farm. Without any fanfare the mail sacks are dumped on a truck and driven back to Washington, to be sent on to Philadelphia and New York by train. A rather embarrassing start for the new airmail service.

To add to the confusion of the day, a printer makes an embarrassing error. The first airmail stamps issued for this flight show Jenny flying upside-down.

In following weeks the outlook brightened. The Jennys flew daily over the 218-mile route between Washington, Philadelphia, and New York City. An average trip took about three-and-one-half hours, and although there were mishaps, a routine was soon established. This was only the beginning. When the mail planes were operating on schedule, plans were laid to fly the mail west to Cleveland and Chicago.

9

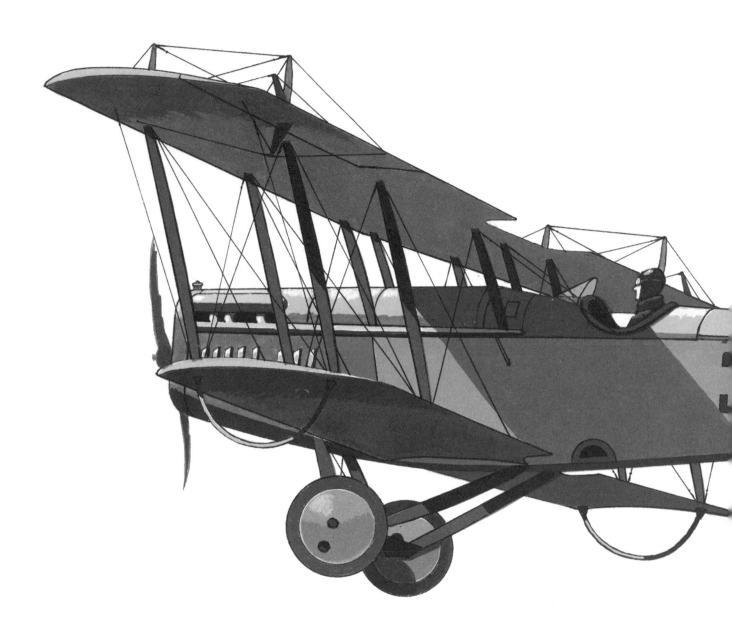

Let's take a closer look at Jenny. She had other work to do besides carry the mail. During World War I she was used to train many Army pilots. After the war she thrilled crowds at county fairs. Excited children and adults watched a daredevil stunt man swing from a trapeze below Jenny's landing gear, then walk her top wing while the pilot put her through hair-raising barrel rolls and inside and outside loops. She became as popular and well known as Henry Ford's "Model T" car.

10

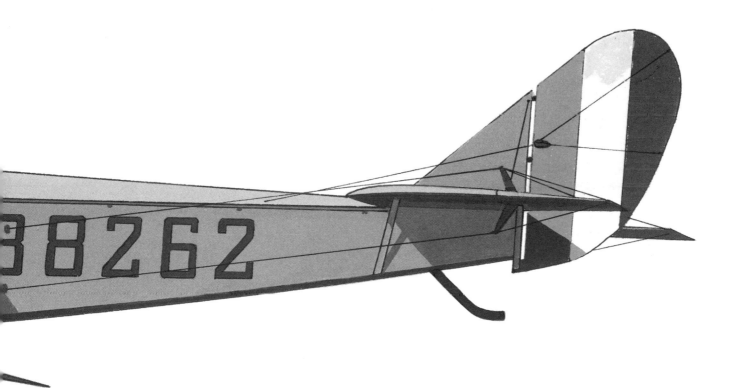

With a "Hisso" engine Jenny's top speed was 93 miles per hour. She could carry 150 pounds of mail for 230 miles and stay up for 2½ hours before she ran low on fuel.

The airmail started with Jenny, but before very long she became outmoded. A larger, more powerful plane was needed when the mail headed westward. Nevertheless, because she was the first to carry the mail over a scheduled route, Jenny can truly be called the grandmother of today's jetliner.

11

CHAPTER TWO

Pony Express in the Sky

Another mail plane enters the picture on September 5, 1918, when the first, trail-blazing flight was made between New York and Chicago. From the Army, the Post Office acquired a number of de Havilland DH-4's. They had been built for World War I and, when remodeled to fly the mail, they could carry up to 400 pounds of cargo. They could carry it faster and for a longer distance without refueling than the Jennys.

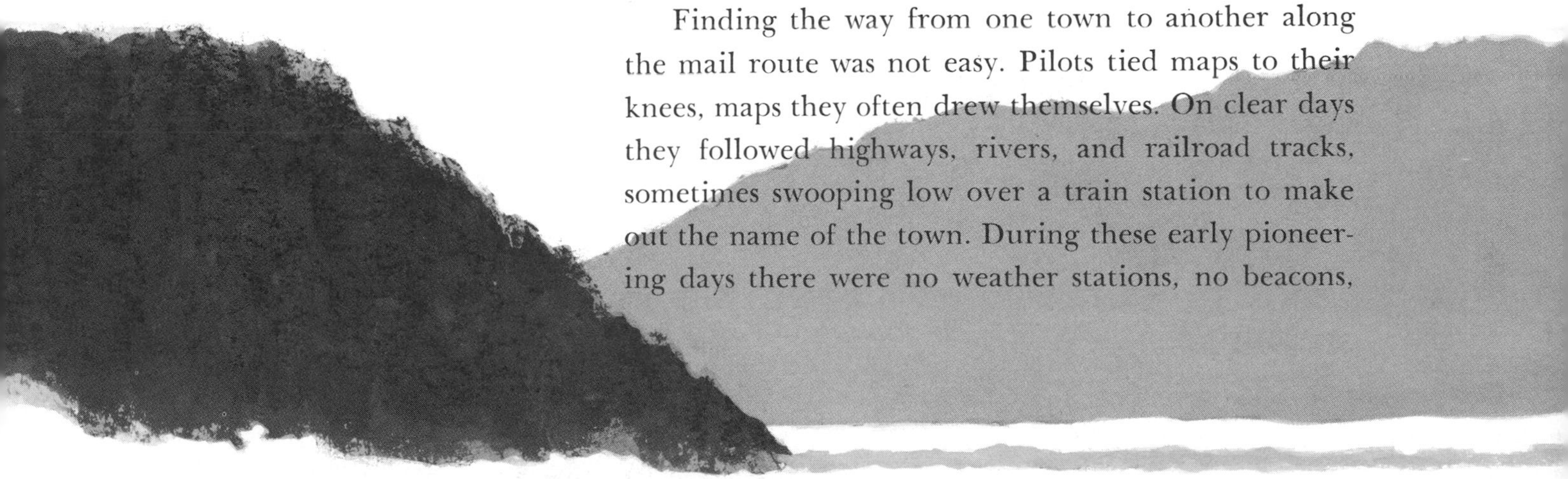

Finding the way from one town to another along the mail route was not easy. Pilots tied maps to their knees, maps they often drew themselves. On clear days they followed highways, rivers, and railroad tracks, sometimes swooping low over a train station to make out the name of the town. During these early pioneering days there were no weather stations, no beacons, no emergency landing fields. The first mail pilots were a stouthearted lot, all alone in the air with no help from anyone on the ground.

But there were some drawbacks. Like the Jenny, the DH-4 had only a few instruments. It had no instruments for flying blind in fog or in a snowstorm, no radio to call the nearest airport for directions or weather information, no landing lights, and no heat at all in the open cockpits.

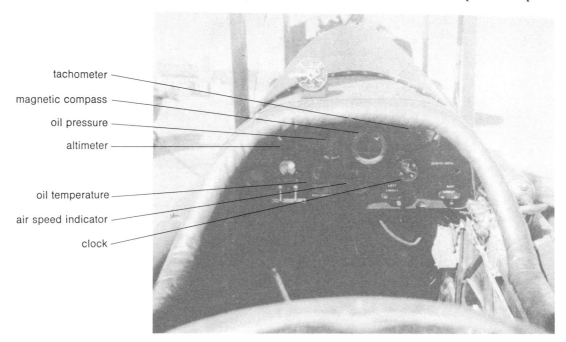

tachometer
magnetic compass
oil pressure
altimeter

oil temperature
air speed indicator
clock

The mail route from New York to Chicago crossed some of the worst flying country in the United States—the Allegheny Mountains. Pilots encountered unpredictable air currents, violent thunderstorms, and fog. Surrounded by fog, a pilot could lose all sense of direction and often they spun out of control. Many lost their lives. Still, day after day, the mail somehow went through.

On May 15, 1920, two years to the day after the start of the airmail service, the route reached Omaha, Nebraska. By September 8 it stretched all the way to the West Coast, as transcontinental service was established between New York and San Francisco. But still the pilots could fly only as long as there was daylight. To keep the mail moving through the night, it had to be transferred to the railroad.

In 1921, on Washington's birthday, the first coast-to-coast flight was completed by flying both day and night over unlighted airways. Two mail planes left New York and two left San Francisco at the same time for the cross-country flight.

The westbound flight was grounded by a snowstorm at Chicago. One of the two eastbound pilots crashed and was killed as he took off from Elko, Nevada. The other eastbound plane made it to North Platte, Nebraska, where Jack Knight, the relief pilot, waited to fly the mail to Omaha. He departed at 10:45 PM not knowing what a long, hazardous night lay ahead. It was bitter cold. Snow was beginning to fall. Arriving at Omaha shortly after 1 AM Knight discovered that his relief pilot had not arrived. Tired and numbed by the cold, Knight nevertheless climbed back into his cockpit and headed out into the darkness for Chicago, a stretch he had not flown before.

Earlier, the attendants at landing fields along the way had built bonfires in an effort to guide the pilots. By now, convinced that all mail planes were grounded, one by one they doused their fires and went to bed.

With the aid of a road map and a flashlight Knight picked his way along the route. Unable to find the darkened landing field at Des Moines, he set his course for Iowa City, another 100 miles away. By now the snow had turned into a blizzard. The engine in Knight's plane began to sputter just as he reached the outskirts of the city. The night watchman alerted and dashed out onto the field to light a flare. Jack Knight landed with only a few drops of gas left in the tank. Once refueled, he was off again and by daybreak he reached Chicago, where another plane took the mail on to New York. Jack Knight was just one of many heroic trailblazers that lived up to the motto of our mail carriers: "Neither snow, nor rain, nor heat, nor gloom of night stays these couriers from the swift completion of their appointed rounds."

16

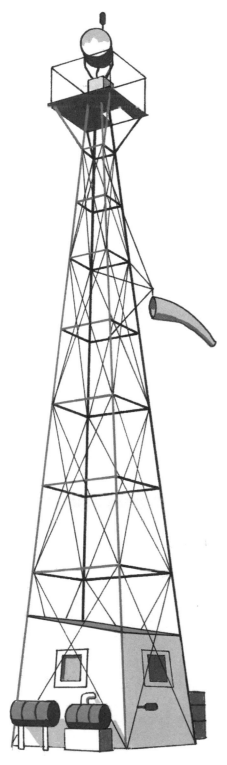

It was clear that if night flying along the transcontinental route were to continue the airways had to be lighted. The Post Office set about immediately installing lights on mail planes. A red light was placed on the left wing tip and a green light on the right wing tip. A white light flashed on the tail. Luminous dials, like watches that glow in the dark, were added to the cockpit. Brilliant landing lights were mounted on the lower wing. The plane carried two parachute flares to help the pilot locate a landing field after dark. When the pilot dropped a flare a little parachute opened. The burning flare, drifting slowly to earth, lighted up the surrounding area for nearly a mile.

By 1924 all the major landing fields were lighted. Each field was equipped with a large revolving beacon. On a clear night the beam could be seen for more than 100 miles. Large floodlights were also used, to assist the pilot during takeoff and landing. The field was outlined with a string of small white lights; red lights marked all obstacles.

Emergency landing fields were located strategically every 25 or 30 miles along the entire route. Each field had a small beacon, a telephone, and a caretaker's shack. Still smaller beacons that were placed every three miles flashed once every second during the night. Now the airmail pilot could follow a highway of lights clear across the country.

17

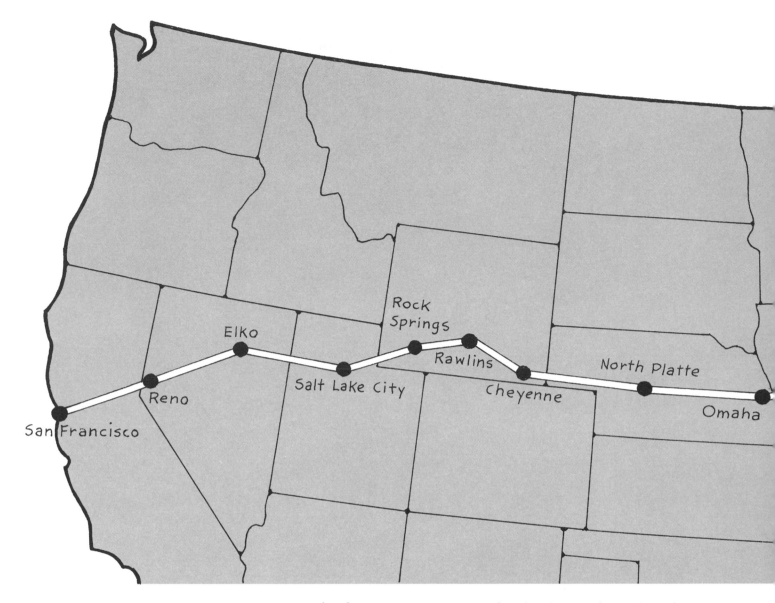

As the pony express traveled in short relays, changing riders and horses, so the airmail was relayed across the country. No pilot or plane flew over 200 miles at a stretch. The mail bags exchanged hands at 14 refueling points scattered along the transcontinental route. Leaving New York, the scheduled stops were Bellefonte, Cleveland, Bryan, Chicago, Iowa City, Omaha, North Platte, Cheyenne, Rawlins, Rock Springs, Salt Lake City, Reno, and San Francisco.

The average time of the westbound New York-to-San Francisco flight was a little over 30 hours, but eastbound flights received a healthy push from a brisk tail wind and made it to New York in about 25 hours, including all stops.

18

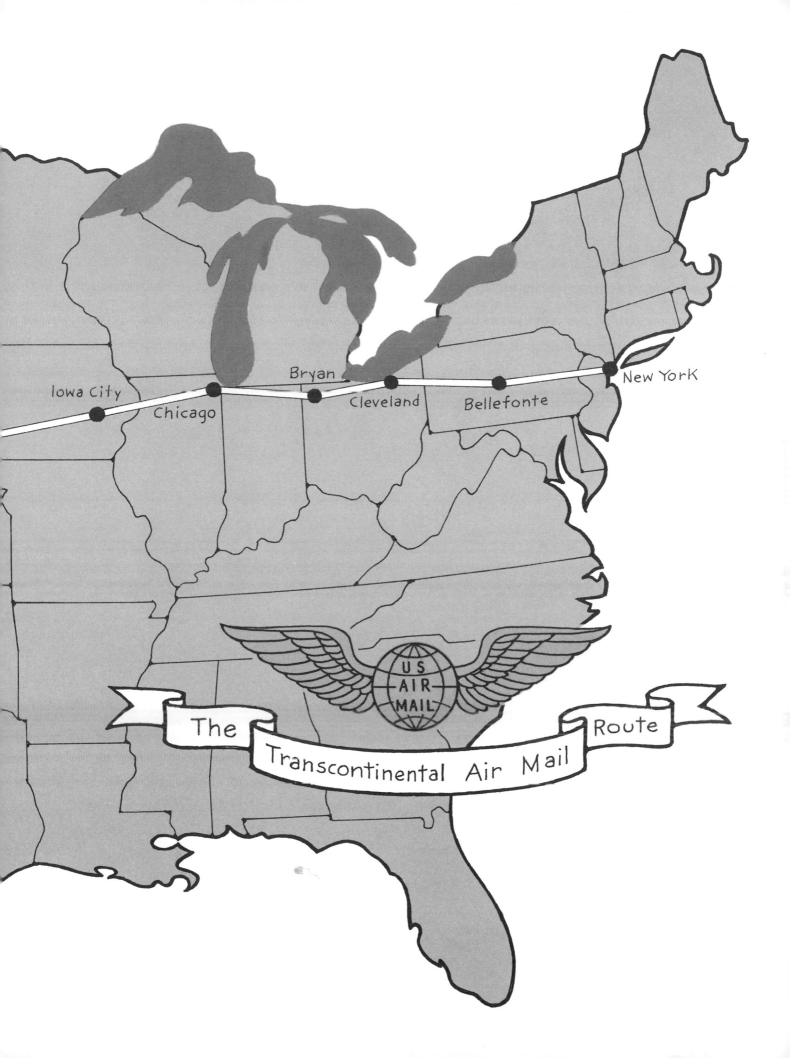

Iowa City

Chicago

Bryan

Cleveland

Bellefonte

New York

US AIR MAIL

The Transcontinental Air Mail Route

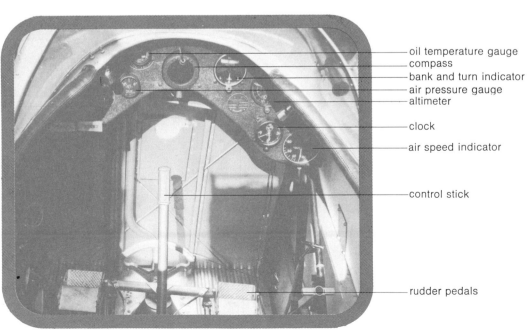

oil temperature gauge
compass
bank and turn indicator
air pressure gauge
altimeter

clock

air speed indicator

control stick

rudder pedals

CHAPTER THREE

Passengers Take to the Skies

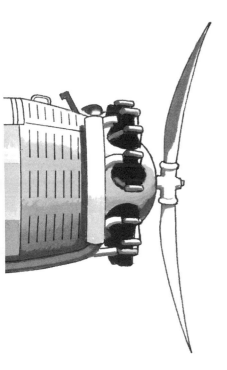

Ever since the airmail service began, the Post Office Department intended someday to turn its routes over to private companies. Now that the mail was flying regularly, day and night, winter and summer, the time seemed ripe. On February 2, 1925, Congress passed the Kelly Bill, "to encourage commercial aviation and authorize the Postmaster General to contract for airmail service."

Later that year the government began awarding airmail contracts, and 12 routes had been handed out to private companies by 1927. Although a few airlines operated before this time, this was the beginning of the airline system as we know it today.

Many of these new companies were not too happy with the prospect of carrying passengers. They knew

they would have to buy larger planes, build passenger terminals, handle baggage, arrive and depart on time, and look after the safety and comfort of their air travelers. Mail sacks never asked annoying questions about delays or complained about planes being grounded because of weather. Transporting the mail remained the airlines' chief concern.

But little by little their attitude toward passengers changed. One of the first planes built to carry both mail and passengers was the Douglas M-2. Entering service in 1926 with a Liberty engine, the Douglas was a husky biplane. Two hatches in front of the pilot were for stowage of mail, but if the mail load were light, one or both of the hatches could be converted to open cockpits. The passengers who would ride there were compelled to struggle into heavy, fur-lined flying suits known as "Teddy bears." They strapped on helmets, goggles, and parachutes. Waddling about like ducks, they waited impatiently while the plane was oiled and gassed, the engine was warmed up, the mail sacks were loaded, and the pilot had his last cup of coffee before taking off. Often these hardy passengers were asked to share their tiny cockpits with the cumbersome mail pouches. Worst of all, if the mail load were heavy the passengers were "bumped" from their flight at the last minute and left stranded on the field. They had to make it back to town somehow and take a train. Small wonder most people thought twice before flying in these early years.

In 1927 the Boeing Model 40-A, while primarily a mail plane, carried two passengers in a cabin sandwiched between two mail compartments. Although the cabin was cramped and quite noisy, the passengers were at least inside, protected from the raw wind, rain, and cold. Reading lights, heat, and ventilation were provided. The pilot, a robust type, preferred to stay outside in an open cockpit battling the elements. It took a while to convince him how much cozier it was inside.

A later model, the Boeing 40-B-4, was equipped with two way radio-phones so the pilot could communicate with airport personnel. These large, single-engine biplanes could

23

carry 1,200 pounds of mail and four passengers at a speed of 125 miles an hour. They were used a number of years on the San Francisco-Chicago run by Boeing Air Transport before that company became United Air Lines.

Newspaper headlines of Lindbergh's spectacular New York to Paris flight in 1927 electrified the nation. This flight, along with other, historic flights by Byrd and Chamberlin, gave aviation the boost it badly needed. Overnight the public became air-minded. Airlines expanded and merged with other airlines to weave an elaborate network of routes across the face of America. As the airlines linked cities they searched for larger, faster, more dependable aircraft. The only answer was to add more engines. The trimotors were born.

The first to take to the skies was the Fokker F-10 in 1927. It was followed quickly by the Ford trimotor. These transports were closely matched in appearance and performance. Each was a high-wing monoplane with three Pratt & Whitney Wasp engines of 425 horsepower. Cruising speed was around 120 miles an hour.

Each had a crew of two, a pilot and a co-pilot. The Fokker F-10 carried 12 passengers; the Ford, 13. But whereas the Fokker trimotor had a wing that was covered with plywood and a fuselage, or body, covered with fabric, the Ford's big advantage was that it was covered from nose to tail with a corrugated metal skin that was extremely strong and durable. The Fokker F-10s faded from the airways in 1932. Thanks to rugged construction, some Fords are flying still.

Fokker produced the huge F-32 in 1929; with four engines, it carried 32 passengers. It was not a success and only a few were built.

A
PORTFOLIO
OF
AIRCRAFT

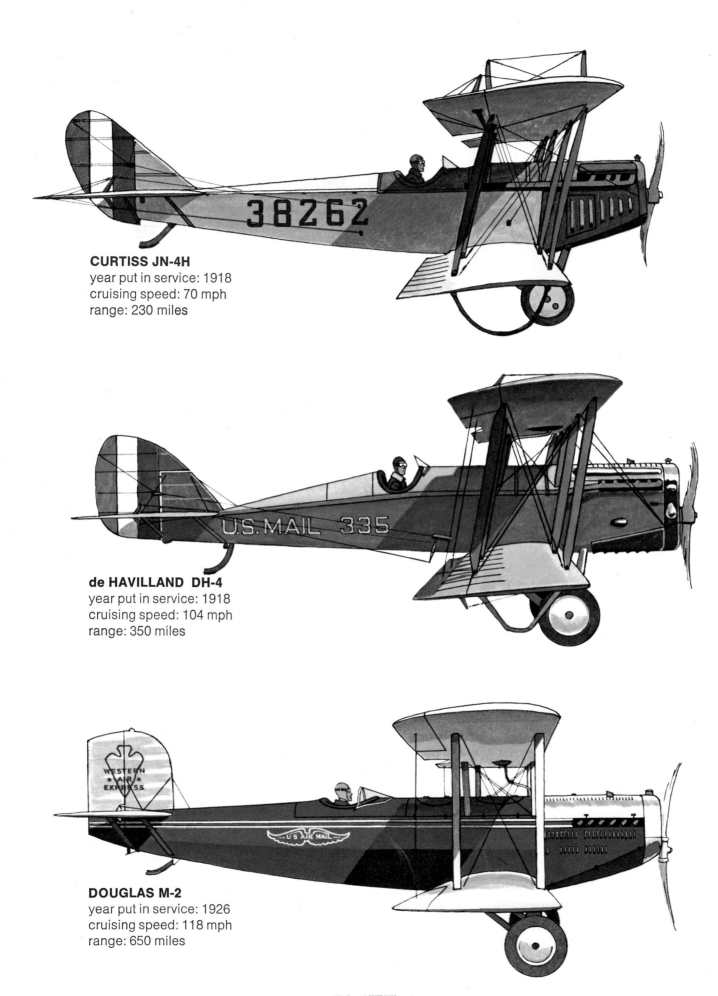

CURTISS JN-4H
year put in service: 1918
cruising speed: 70 mph
range: 230 miles

de HAVILLAND DH-4
year put in service: 1918
cruising speed: 104 mph
range: 350 miles

DOUGLAS M-2
year put in service: 1926
cruising speed: 118 mph
range: 650 miles

PLATE 1

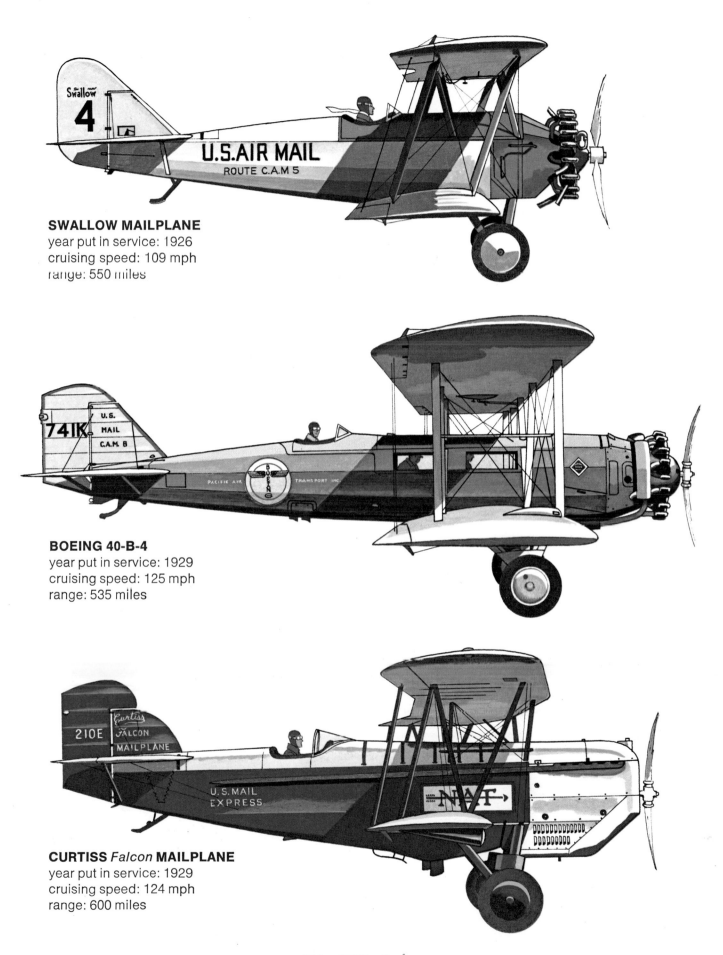

SWALLOW MAILPLANE
year put in service: 1926
cruising speed: 109 mph
range: 550 miles

BOEING 40-B-4
year put in service: 1929
cruising speed: 125 mph
range: 535 miles

CURTISS *Falcon* **MAILPLANE**
year put in service: 1929
cruising speed: 124 mph
range: 600 miles

PLATE 2

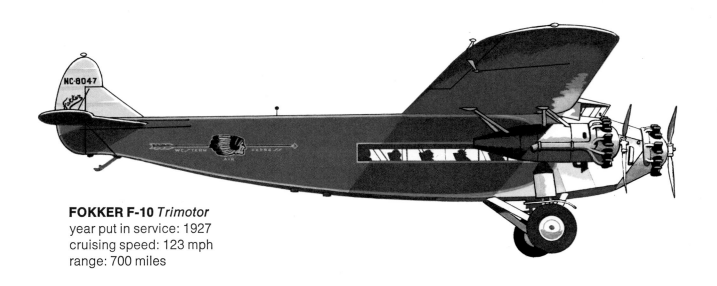

FOKKER F-10 *Trimotor*
year put in service: 1927
cruising speed: 123 mph
range: 700 miles

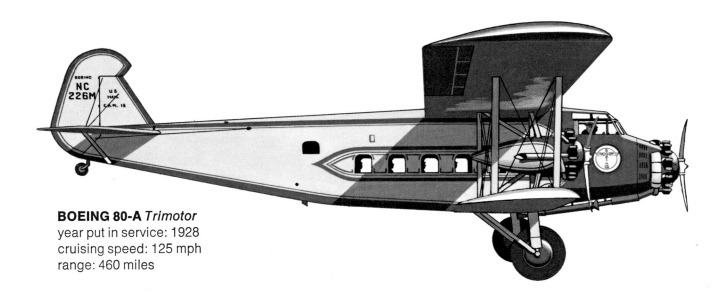

BOEING 80-A *Trimotor*
year put in service: 1928
cruising speed: 125 mph
range: 460 miles

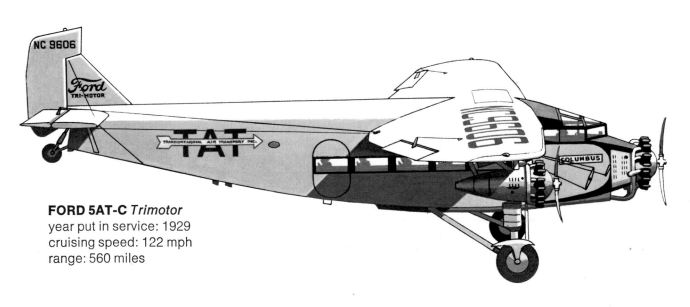

FORD 5AT-C *Trimotor*
year put in service: 1929
cruising speed: 122 mph
range: 560 miles

PLATE 3

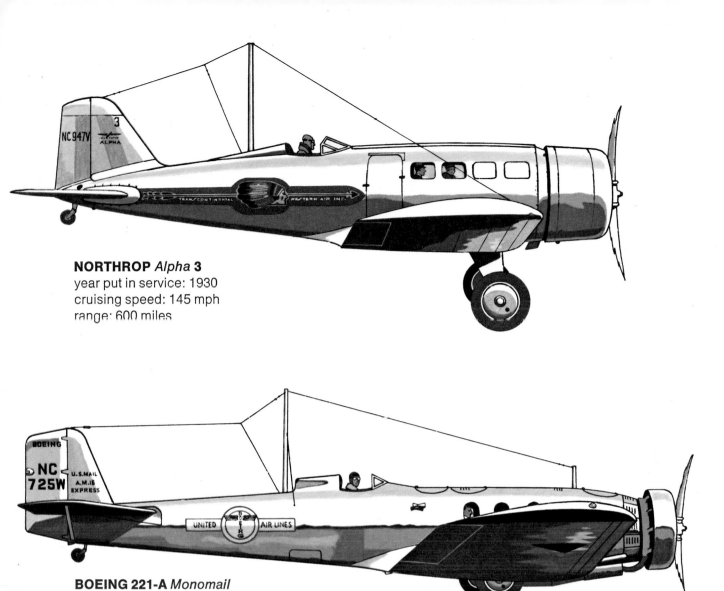

NORTHROP *Alpha* **3**
year put in service: 1930
cruising speed: 145 mph
range: 600 miles

BOEING 221-A *Monomail*
year put in service: 1930
cruising speed: 137 mph
range: 540 miles

LOCKHEED 9 *Orion*
year put in service: 1931
cruising speed: 180 mph
range: 720 miles

PLATE 4

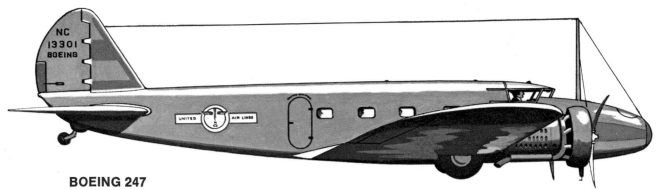

BOEING 247
year put in service: 1933
cruising speed: 155 mph
range: 485 miles

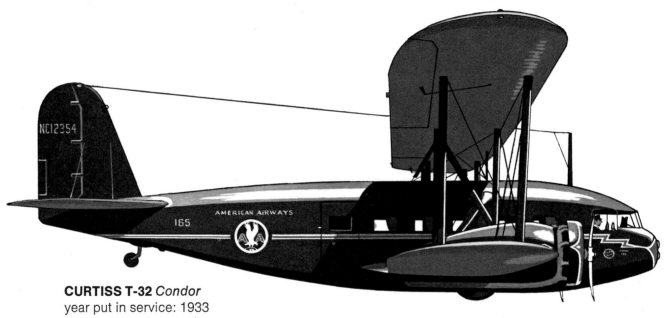

CURTISS T-32 *Condor*
year put in service: 1933
cruising speed: 152 mph
range: 650 miles

DOUGLAS DC-1
year put in service: 1933
cruising speed: 184 mph
range: 515 miles

PLATE 5

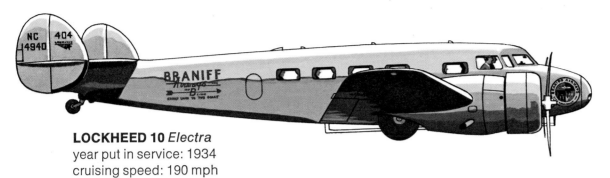

LOCKHEED 10 *Electra*
year put in service: 1934
cruising speed: 190 mph
range: 850 miles

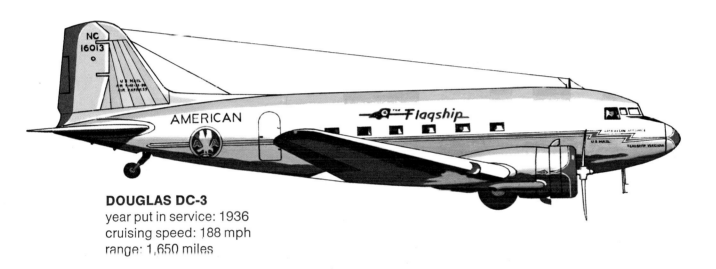

DOUGLAS DC-3
year put in service: 1936
cruising speed: 188 mph
range: 1,650 miles

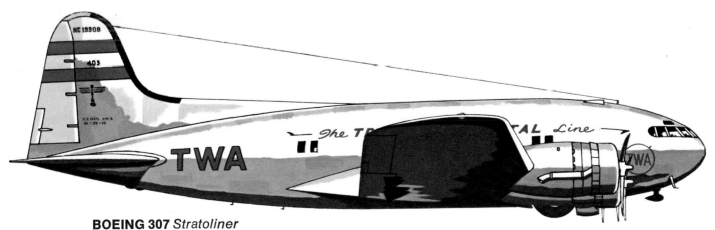

BOEING 307 *Stratoliner*
year put in service: 1940
cruising speed: 220 mph
range: 2,390 miles

PLATE 6

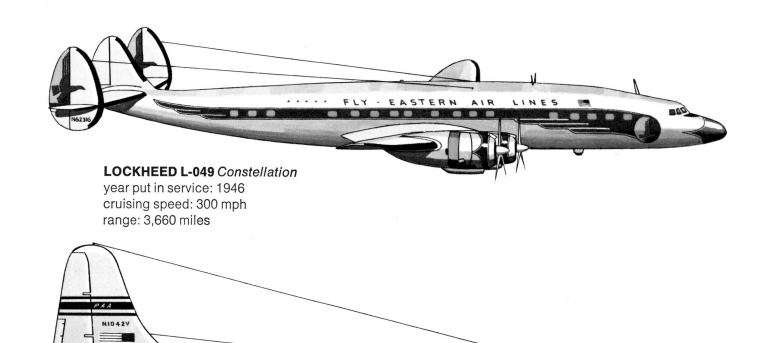

LOCKHEED L-049 *Constellation*
year put in service: 1946
cruising speed: 300 mph
range: 3,660 miles

BOEING 377 *Stratocruiser*
year put in service: 1949
cruising speed: 340 mph
range: 4,200 miles

DOUGLAS DC-7
year put in service: 1954
cruising speed: 365 mph
range: 4,415 miles

PLATE 7

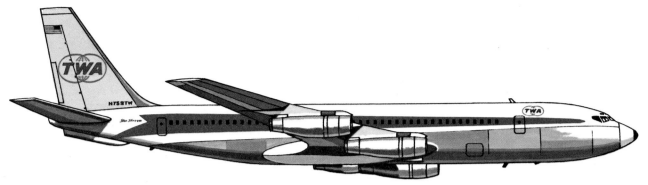

BOEING 707
year put in service: 1954
cruising speed: 571 mph
range: 3,075 miles

DOUGLAS DC-8
year put in service: 1958
cruising speed: 550 mph
range: 5,700 miles

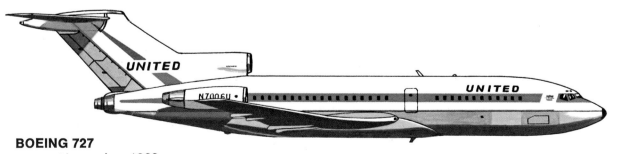

BOEING 727
year put in service: 1963
cruising speed: 596 mph
range: 3,430 miles

PLATE 8

CURTISS JN-4

FORD *Trimotor*

DOUGLAS DC-3

LOCKHEED *Super Constellation*

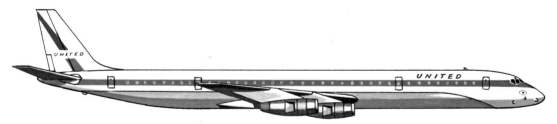

BOEING 707

DOUGLAS *Super* **DC-8**

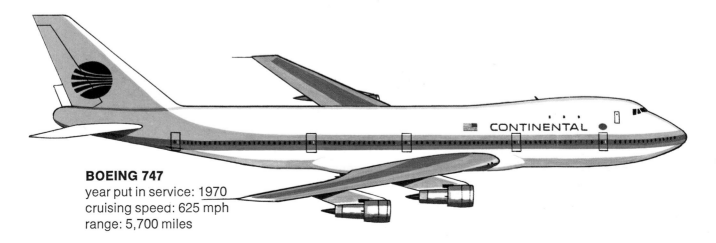

BOEING 747
year put in service: 1970
cruising speed: 625 mph
range: 5,700 miles

PLATE 9

McDONNELL DOUGLAS DC-10
year put in service: 1971
cruising speed: 600 mph
range: 3,670 miles

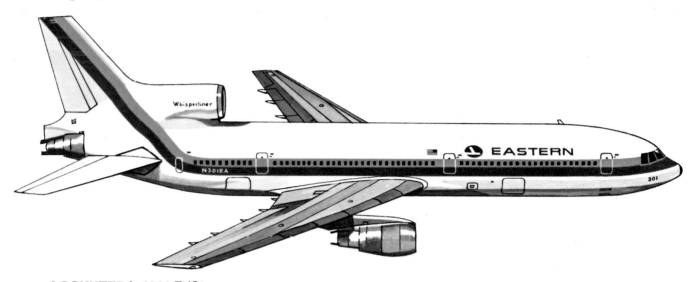

LOCKHEED L-1011 *TriStar*
year put in service: 1972
cruising speed: 600 mph
range: 3,511 miles

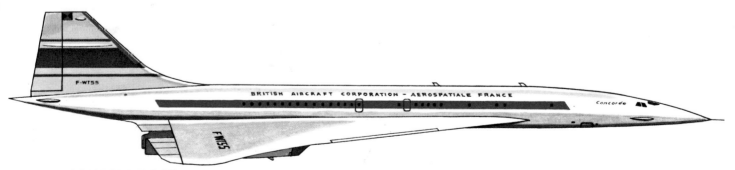

CONCORDE SST
cruising speed: 1,400 mph
range: 4,000 miles

PLATE 10

CHAPTER FOUR

Coast to Coast in a Ford Trimotor

Today you can fly nonstop from New York to Los Angeles in four-and-one-half hours, leaving New York in the morning and arriving on the Coast before lunch.

In 1929 the fastest travel time one could expect between New York and Los Angeles was 48 hours—and at least half that time was spent on a train! Passenger planes didn't fly at night, and it was considered too dangerous, even in the daytime, to fly passengers over the Alleghenies and the Rocky Mountains. Still, crossing the country in 48 hours left the public absolutely giddy in 1929; after all, the fastest train took at least four days.

Two airlines, TAT (Transcontinental Air Transport) and Maddux, and two railways, the Pennsylvania and the Santa Fe, provided the schedule that made the

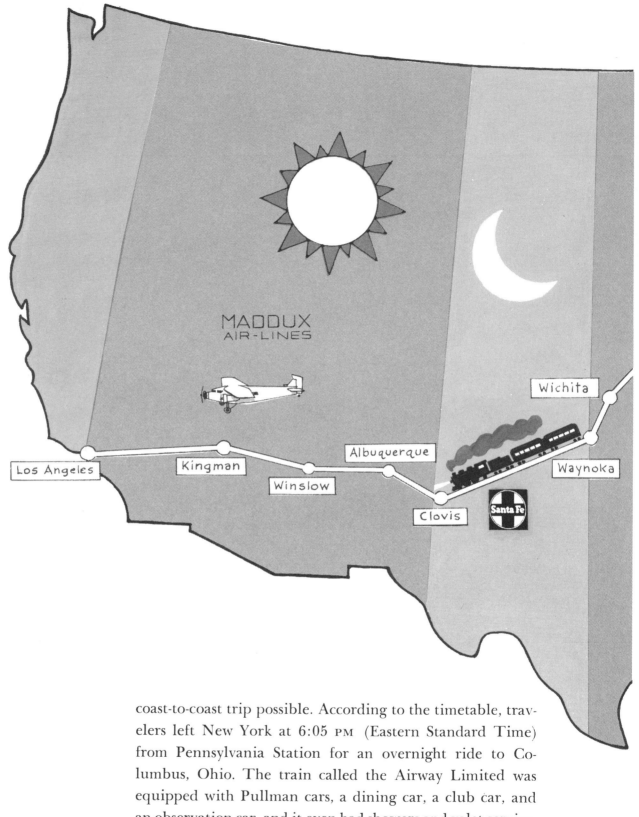

coast-to-coast trip possible. According to the timetable, travelers left New York at 6:05 PM (Eastern Standard Time) from Pennsylvania Station for an overnight ride to Columbus, Ohio. The train called the Airway Limited was equipped with Pullman cars, a dining car, a club car, and an observation car, and it even had showers and valet service.

At Port Columbus (Ohio) the passengers boarded a Ford trimotor and at 7:35 in the morning started winging their way over midwestern farms. After stops at Indianapolis, St. Louis, Kansas City, and Wichita they arrived at Way-

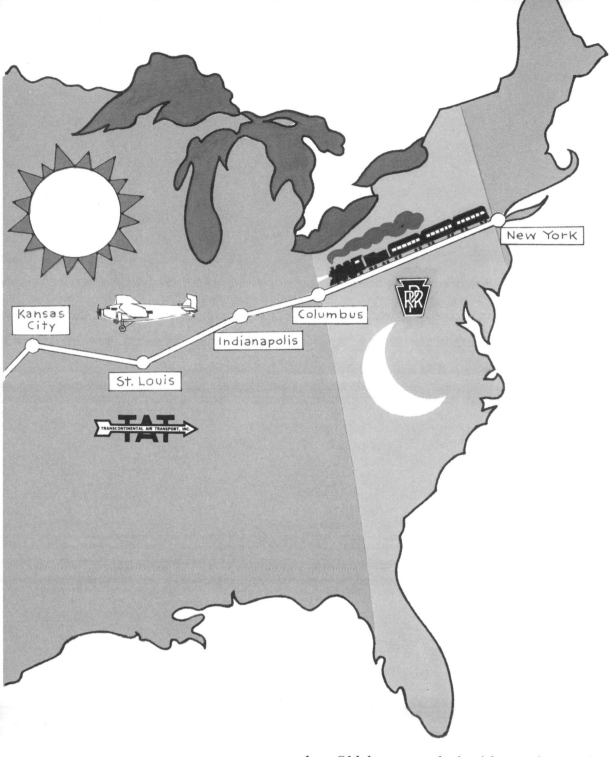

noka, Oklahoma, at dusk. After a four-and-one-half-hour layover here they departed on a Santa Fe train for the overnight trip to Clovis, New Mexico. At 8:10 AM (Mountain Time), an hour after their arrival at Clovis, the passengers were airborne again. They flew over desert areas and made stops at Albuquerque, Winslow, and Kingman, finally putting down at Los Angeles at 4:30 (Pacific Standard Time) that afternoon. The eastbound flight was slightly shorter.

27

Passengers made the first trip from New York to Los Angeles entirely by air in 1930. The plane, a Ford trimotor, followed basically the same route as our earlier journey, and the flight took 36 hours with scheduled stops. Although 12 hours was snipped off the previous time, passengers still spent the night on good old solid earth, this time in Kansas City.

What was it like to fly in a Ford trimotor? To the adventuresome gadabouts of 1929 the Ford trimotor was the last word in modern transportation. It was of all-metal construction. It had a top speed of 140 miles an hour and could fly a distance of 550 to 600 miles or about four-and-one-half hours without refueling. It was a very stable airplane. For the first time commercial flying became popular, and an important reason was that air passengers finally felt safe in a Ford trimotor.

Let's take a short trip in this famous old aircraft. Approaching the cabin door we notice that the pilot no longer sits outside but, with a co-pilot, is in an enclosed cockpit. We see large compartments under the wings and we are told that's where the mail bags are stowed. You won't have to share your cabin with them or hold them in your lap. When we board, we are struck by the fact that the cabin looks a good deal smaller inside than it does outside; it's hard to believe that it actually holds 13 people.

As we fasten our seatbelts and taxi down the runway we become sharply aware of the deafening roar erupting from the three engines. The co-pilot comes back with wads of cotton for our ears and chewing gum to relieve the air pressure. We soon find that talking to each other across the aisle is next to impossible.

Once in the air the trimotor starts to shake and rattle as if it were throwing a fit. On top of all this we detect a faint odor of exhaust fumes seeping into the cabin and the so-called heating system leaves something to be desired for a cold draft starts blowing about our ankles.

Lumbering along at 120 miles an hour we glance out the window and realize how low the pilot is flying. He stays well

beneath the clouds and does not lose sight of the ground. He still navigates by identifying familiar landmarks. Flying low also makes it easier for him to pick out an emergency landing field if we should need fuel or repairs, or if the weather should turn bad. These small dilemmas did spring up from time to time.

By now it is lunchtime. There's no stewardess, so the co-pilot, doubling as waiter, comes down the narrow aisle serving a box lunch to each passenger. Inside the box we find an apple, a cold chicken or ham sandwich, and a cookie for dessert.

Soon we arrive at our destination and once more our feet touch on firm ground. Our ears are still ringing and we are inclined to wobble from side to side as we make our way to the terminal. I'm sure you will agree that this way of traveling is a far cry from the swift, comfortable jetliners of today. Nevertheless, the Ford trimotor was the most reliable transport of its day. Its safety record was so good that nearly 200 models were built and they were flown by every major airline in the United States.

CHAPTER FIVE

Flying Becomes Faster and Safer

At first the airlines had no taste for night flying. It was true that on a clear evening you could travel down a lighted highway guided by a string of glowing beacons, but when fog crept in and blanketed the earth below it was a different, often tragic story. To make night flying safer for pilots and passengers the radio beam was developed.

When fog blots out the beacon lights, the pilot listens through his earphones to the signals coming from the airport's beacon transmitter. As long as he is on course—"on the beam"—he hears a steady hum. If he drifts to one side of the beam he hears a dot-dash sound—an "A" in Morse code. If he drifts to the opposite side he hears a dash-dot sound—an "N" in Morse code. Every so often the hum is interrupted to give

33

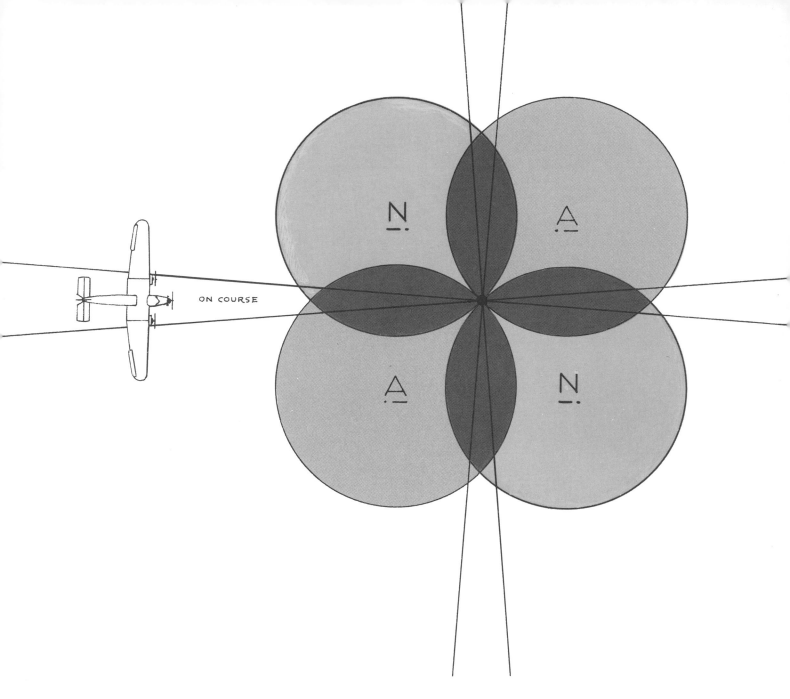

ON COURSE

N ▲ ▲ N

the pilot the time and weather information. This invisible radio beam was the first major step to help the pilot battle the deadly enemy of fog.

As flying became faster and safer, the airlines looked for ways to transport their growing passenger traffic. The Boeing Company, seeing a need for a larger transport than their four-passenger model 40, produced the model 80 in 1928. This three-engine, 18-passenger biplane helped whittle the transcontinental travel time down to 27 hours. The heated cabin of the Boeing 80 boasted unheard-of luxuries—

leather seats, a lavatory with hot and cold running water, forced-air ventilation, reading lights, and soundproofing. The noise level was finally lowered to a point where it was possible to carry on conversations with other passengers.

In 1930 the first stewardess was introduced on this airliner. Her duties were those the co-pilot had always grudgingly attended to: making the passengers comfortable, pointing out places of interest, and serving meals. Air travelers heartily approved of this new member of the crew and soon other airlines were hiring and training young women to serve on their transports.

Something new appeared in the western sky in 1930—a sleek, all-metal, low-wing transport that forecast the shape of things to come. It was the single-engine Boeing Monomail, carrying 8 passengers and 750 pounds of mail. To increase its air speed after takeoff, the Monomail tucked its wheels neatly into its thick wing, allowing the air to flow smoothly over the wing's surface. Retracting the landing gear in this way is now standard practice on all large transports.

One feature of the Boeing Monomail was a throwback
to earlier days: the pilot sat outside in an open cockpit.
Several other transports still had open cockpits in 1930—the
Lockheed Air Express, the Consolidated Fleetster, and the
Northrop Alpha. Some hardy airline pilots needed a lot
of coaxing to get them inside the cabin.

The design of the Monomail soon led to our first truly
modern airliner, the Boeing 247. Advertised as the "3-mile-
a-minute" transport, the Boeing 247 was an all-metal, low-
wing, twin-engine design with retractable landing gear.
Wing de-icers and heating controlled by a thermostat were
introduced on this plane that accommodated 10 passengers

and a crew of three: pilot, co-pilot, and stewardess. Entering service in 1933, the Boeing 247 trimmed nearly one-third off the old coast-to-coast time of 27 hours, making the run with seven stops in 19½ hours. Its top speed was 186 miles an hour—almost 50 miles an hour faster than the old tri-motors, and the Boeing 247 was able to climb with a full load on only one of its engines.

Following closely on the heels of the Boeing design was the low-wing, twin-engine Douglas DC-1. A larger aircraft than the Boeing 247, the Douglas held 12 passengers. Each of her two Wright Cyclone engines developed 710 horsepower and the new airliner had a maximum speed of 210 miles an hour.

The last of the biplane transports was the twin-engine Curtiss Condor of 1933. Two versions were in use: a standard daytime type that seated 15 and a sleeper with berths for 12. The Curtiss Condor cruised at 152 miles an hour. Although the speed was rather sluggish, the flights were always quiet and comfortable.

The next year saw the arrival of a new member of the Douglas family, the DC-2, with room for 14 passengers and a top speed of 213 miles an hour. New features the DC-2 could boast of included an automatic pilot (a device that under favorable conditions could take over the pilot's job and fly the plane), wheel brakes, a galley equipped with a refrigerator for serving meals aloft, and controllable-pitch propellers (a feature that allowed the pilot to change the angle of the propeller blade while in flight to take a larger bite out of the air).

The year 1934 also saw the introduction of the Lockheed 10 Electra. Smaller and faster than the Boeing and Douglas models, this twin-tailed transport carried eight passengers and a crew of two, at speeds up to 221 miles an hour.

The transcontinental flight time was bettered once again in 1936 when the Douglas DC-3 burst upon the scene. The large, plump sister of the DC-2 carried 21 passengers and flew coast to coast in only 17 hours.

Originally the DC-3 had sleeping berths for 14 people and was known as the Douglas DST-Douglas Sleeper Transport. These new Douglas Flagships, as they were called, replaced the old Curtiss Condors for American Airlines. Now a traveler could leave Los Angeles late in the afternoon, enjoy a pleasant night's sleep in a Pullman-style berth, and arrive refreshed in New York the following morning. Flagships were also equipped with separate dressing rooms for men and women and a private drawing room. Meals were served on tables with linen, silverware, and fine china. All this was an attempt to match the luxury and glamour of the crack express trains. For added comfort the airliners were air-conditioned.

All the major airlines scrambled to replace their old equipment with the popular new transport. The Douglas DC-3 became the leading airliner in the nation. Large orders even poured in from overseas.

With the outbreak of World War II in Europe the DC-3 was drafted. Douglas built over 10,000 DC-3s for the Allied Forces, and they were put to work carrying troops and cargo. It is estimated that there are still over 1,000 DC-3s in active airline service today, 33 years after its first flight.

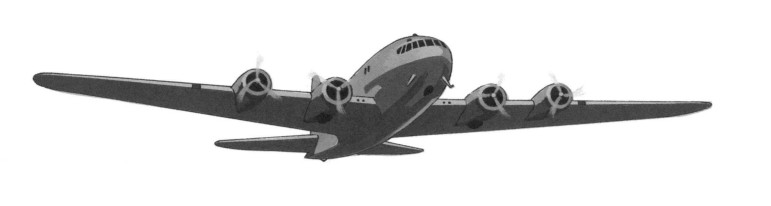

CHAPTER SIX

Flight of the Four-engine Giants

Until the Boeing Stratoliner came along in 1940, airline pilots facing rough weather along their routes had little choice but to fly through it. The new stratoliner, with the added power of four engines and a "pressurized" cabin, could climb up above the storm clouds to where the air was much smoother. Pressurizing the cabin allowed passengers to breathe normally although flying three or four miles above the earth. The Stratoliner carried 33 passengers and had five crew members; a pilot, a co-pilot, a flight engineer with his own set of instruments, and two stewardesses. Coast-to-coast time was cut down to 14 hours.

Douglas launched a new series of giants with the DC-4, the first airliner to have three landing wheels— a tricycle landing gear. The DC-4 cruised at 230 miles an hour and carried between 44 and 60 passengers. Because of the war she didn't see airline service until 1946. By then the larger DC-6 was already hopping from coast to coast above the weather in nine-and-one-half hours.

About this time Lockheed reentered the race with the four-engine Constellation. Designed before the war and used as a military transport, "Connie" came to the airlines in 1946. This graceful transport matched the speed of the DC-6 at more than 300 miles an hour. With the Constellation, TWA and Pan American Airways introduced round-the-world flights in 1947.

Boeing based its next model, the Stratocruiser, on the B-29 Superfortress bomber. The huge double-deck airliner produced in 1949 carried up to 112 passengers on two levels. The seven crew members included the regular staff plus a navigator and a radio operator. Cruising at 340 miles an hour, the Stratocruiser flew the Tokyo-to-Seattle run in 17 hours with only one refueling stop.

In 1950 the Lockheed Constellation acquired new high-altitude turbo-charged engines. The cabin was stretched 18 feet to make room for 63 first-class or 100 coach passengers. This Super Constellation made the first nonstop flights between Los Angeles and New York on a regular eight-hour schedule in 1951.

The DC-7, bearing a striking resemblance to the older, four-engine members of the Douglas family, traveled from coast to coast in seven-and-one-half hours in 1954 and flew nonstop from New York to many large cities in Europe. The Douglas DC-7 has the distinction of being the last of the great propeller-driven transports.

CHAPTER SEVEN

Dawn of the Jetliner

A strange new voice was heard in the early 1950s. It was something between a snarl, a screech, and the sound made by whistling through your teeth. The culprit, of course, was the jet transport and with its arrival a magic new era of travel began.

America's first jetliner was the Boeing 707. It took to the skies in 1954 and changed everyone's idea of what a transport plane should look like. Its nose was shaped like a bullet. Wings and tail were swept back at a rakish angle and the jet engines were carried in four separate pods slung under the wing.

The shape of the airliner was radically changed, and now all of the old airline timetables had to be rewritten. The new Boeing could travel at speeds up to 600 miles an hour, a good 200 miles an hour faster than

47

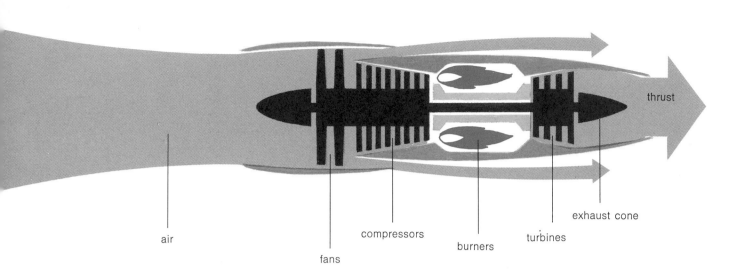

air

fans

compressors

burners

turbines

exhaust cone

thrust

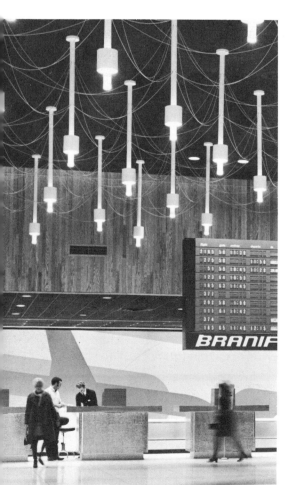

propeller-driven transports. The 707 started flying nonstop from New York to London in 1958 and entered transcontinental service in 1959.

Douglas was the next company to hop on the jet-age bandwagon. Their DC-8 arrived in 1958 and followed closely the outline of the 707. A stretched version, the Super DC-8, entered service in 1966. It employs six stewardesses to look after 251 passengers.

In 1959 a third company produced a jet transport, Convair's medium-range model 880. It flew 615 miles an hour, the fastest cruising speed of any of the larger jets. A sister ship, the 990, appeared in 1961; it is 10 feet longer than the 880.

The next group of jet transports were of medium and short range. Three of these are now in airline service: the Boeing 727, with three engines, and the Boeing 737 and Douglas DC-9, each with two engines. These medium-sized transports are ideal for intercity trips because they are able to take off and land at smaller airports.

Today it seems that everyone is on the go and the air is alive with transport planes. What's to keep them from running into each other? How is all this traffic controlled?

48

Even though you can't see them the paths that airliners fly from city to city are much like our superhighways. Instead of road signs there are many checkpoints along the route where signals are beamed to the airliner by radio stations. The pilot checks his airway chart to locate his exact position and find the distance to the next station.

Airliners, however, fly at different levels so one highway is stacked on top of another. Any aircraft above or below you is at least 1,000 feet away. The nearest one on either side of you is 5 miles away. Another airliner sharing the same highway stays 10 miles ahead of you or behind you and is going the same way. All aerial highways are one-way streets.

Jetliners are built for high altitudes. Flying as high as six miles above the earth, they follow the upper levels and leave the lower highways to the propeller-driven transports.

Control towers at large airports guide the airliner during its flight by radar screens, radio, and computers. From the moment of takeoff until it reaches its destination the airliner never loses contact with the air traffic control on the ground.

With the arrival of the Boeing 747 in 1970 we entered the age of the "superjets." The 747 is the largest commercial plane in the sky. It weighs more than twice the weight of a Boeing 707. This spacious airliner has a range of 5,700 miles and carries up to 490 passengers at a cruising speed of 625 miles per hour.

Two of the newest supersize jetliners are the Lockheed L-1011 and the DC-10 built by McDonnell Douglas. Each has three modern jet engines that permit a cruising speed of about 600 miles per hour. Advanced engine technology will ensure quiet, clean performance.

The world shrinks a little more each time a new jetliner takes to the skies. Tomorrow supersonic transports will speed across our country in two hours or leap across the Atlantic ocean in two-and-one-half hours, devouring space at the incredible rate of 1,800 miles an hour.

When you think of all the progress we have made and what fascinating things the future holds in store, it is hard to believe air travel began such a short time ago with a sputtering little yellow biplane called Jenny.

MAJOR EVENTS IN THE HISTORY OF AIR TRAVEL

1918 First airmail flight, New York–Philadelphia–Washington, D.C.

First New York–Chicago airmail flight.

1920 Airmail route extended to San Francisco (using railroads at night).

1921 First day-and-night flight coast to coast.

1923 Army pilots make first nonstop flight coast to coast.

1924 All major landing fields now lighted for night approaches and takeoffs.

1925 Congress passes the Kelly Bill "to encourage commercial aviation. . . ."

1926 Douglas M-2 carries mail *and* passengers.

1927 Beginning of modern airlines system; 12 mail routes contracted with private companies.

Boeing 40-A flies mail and passengers.

Lindbergh flies nonstop, New York to Paris.

1928 Boeing 80 cuts transcontinental flight time to 24 hours.

1929 Fokker develops the trimotor; Ford follows.

Travel time, New York to Los Angeles: 48 hours.

1930 First stewardess serves in the Boeing 80 trimotor. This plane also has first retractable landing gear.

1933 Boeing builds the 247, the first truly modern airliner; transcontinental travel time: 19½ hours.

Curtiss Condor enters service, one model has berths for sleeping.

1934 Douglas DC-2 has first automatic pilot, controllable pitch propellers.

Lockheed introduces the Electra, sleek twin-tailed transport.

1936 Douglas DC-3 shortens coast-to-coast time to 17 hours; with sleeper berths, luxury service, and air conditioning.

1940 Four-engine Boeing Stratoliner adds first pressurized cabin; flies coast to coast in only 14 hours.

1941 War interrupts the growth of passenger service, and many big planes are used for troops and cargo for war.

1946 Douglas DC-4, developed in 1940, has "tricycle" landing gear.

Douglas DC-6 makes coast-to-coast flight in 9½ hours. Lockheed's new four-engine liner is the Constellation, designed as a troop transport.

51

1947   Constellation inaugurates round-the-world flights for TWA and Pan American.

1949   Boeing adapts its war-time Superfortress for passenger service. The double-deck Stratocruiser flies from Seattle to Tokyo in 17 hours with one stop.

1950   Lockheed's Constellation, with new turbo-charged engines, becomes Super Constellation.

1951   Super Constellation makes first regularly-scheduled nonstop flights between Los Angeles and New York.

1954   Four-engine Douglas DC-7 makes nonstop trips from New York to many large cities in Europe. This plane is the last propeller-driven transport. The same year brings the Boeing 707, the first great jet transport; its speed: 600 miles per hour.

1958   Douglas DC-8, the next jet transport, is put into service.

1959   Convair's 880 is introduced; it cruises at 615 miles per hour.

1961   Convair's 990 is built, and during the 1960s three medium and short-range jets are developed: the three-engine Boeing 727, the two-engine 737, and the Douglas DC-9.

1970   Boeing's giant 747 brings on the age of the "Superjets." The largest commercial plane carries 490 passengers and has a range of 5,700 miles.

1972   Two new giant planes are put into service. Lockheed's L-1011 carries about 200 passengers, as does the McDonnell-Douglas DC-10. Each has three jet engines.

CREDITS

Photo credits
Air Force Museum, Dayton, Ohio, page 14.
American Airlines, pages 25, 37.
Ford Archives, Henry Ford Museum, Dearborn, Mich., page 31.
Smithsonian Institution, pages 2-3, 15, 17, 24, 28, 40 (top).
Trans World Airlines, page 50.
United Air Lines, pages 16, 20, 22, 35, 36, 44 (top).
United Press International, pages 23, 24 (top), 40, 45, 48, 49, 50.
United States Information Agency, pages 41, 44.

Book design
Willis Proudfoot